SOLO CLASSICAL ELECTRIC GUITAR

Iconic & Modern Pieces Arranged for Solo Guitar, Including Bach, Paganini, Chopin & More

ROB THORPE

FUNDAMENTAL CHANGES

Solo Classical Electric Guitar

Iconic & Modern Pieces Arranged for Solo Guitar, Including Bach, Paganini, Chopin & More

ISBN: 978-1-78933-434-0

Published by **www.fundamental-changes.com**

Edited by Joseph Alexander

www.fundamental-changes.com

@robthorpemusic

@fundamentalchanges

Join our free Facebook Community of Cool Musicians

www.facebook.com/groups/fundamentalguitar

For over 350 free guitar lessons with Videos, check out:

www.fundamental-changes.com

Contents

Introduction

"Behold, Electric Guitar!" – Paul Gilbert

The electric guitar is an incredible musical instrument and one that I am passionate about. It's expressive and capable of a wide range of sounds and effects, and as guitarists we can fit into many different musical environments, from jazz to rock, from blues to musical theatre.

However, traditionally, the electric guitar has *always* been an ensemble instrument and normally exists within the holy trinity of guitar, bass and drums.

Playing with other musicians is rewarding and helps us learn a great deal about our art. However, this is not always possible and takes much organisation, coordination and commitment.

There is a wealth of resources available to help the lone guitarist approximate the experience of playing in a band, through jam-tracks and play-along versions of famous songs. These are, of course, beneficial and fun to use. But solo performances can often offer a more profound connection with our audience, with a sense of intimacy and honesty.

Would Jimi Hendrix's legendary rendition of *The Star-Spangled Banner* at Woodstock in 1969 have had the same impact if his band had joined in? Would Jeff Beck's *Where Were You* be as haunting with a rhythm section plodding along behind? Probably not! The nakedness of the solo guitar was integral to both these performances.

Other instruments have a long tradition of solo performance. In particular, the piano and classical guitar enjoy a library of solo repertoire dating back several hundred years, and to suit every ability, from beginner to virtuoso. When an electric rock guitarist performs unaccompanied, the classical approach is often referenced to some degree. Steve Vai's *Eugene's Trick Bag*, for example, or John Petrucci's solo spot from Dream Theater's live album *Once in a LIVEtime,* both assimilate portions of violin pieces into a performance for solo guitar.

Yet, there is a lack of solo material that translates well onto the electric guitar, so this book offers a collection of pieces that are satisfying to perform on electric guitar without backing tracks. Some are direct transcriptions of single-note classical pieces for violin, cello or flute. Others are guitar arrangements of piano pieces.

While players like Joe Pass made solo electric guitar an artform using the chord-melody approach that works equally well on acoustic guitar, here I wanted to retain the signature techniques of modern electric guitar – bending, distortion, volume swells, tapping, harmonics, use of the whammy bar, and electronic effects – to create unaccompanied pieces that were specifically *electric* guitar. Spatial effects such as delay, reverb and sustain, along with loop pedals, are great tools to help the guitar sound bigger in a solo context. Some of these pieces call for such effects, but I've kept their use to a minimum to keep them accessible.

The pieces in this book are taken from the classical tradition, which has a very different approach to playing "time" than popular music. To *groove*, popular music's pulse should be rock solid with the whole band perfectly locking in with a grid of subdivisions. In classical music, the pulse is allowed to ebb and flow, speeding up as the music intensifies and slowing down as it relaxes. This use of expressive changes in tempo is called *rubato* (literally "stolen time").

To make the pieces in this book more expressive and stylistic, experiment with *rubato,* melodic phrasing, and dynamics. The tuition notes for each piece might recommend speeding up or slowing down in certain places, but I encourage you to create your own personal interpretations.

Expert Insight

To prepare this book, I interviewed three professional classical instrumentalists who give valuable insight and expertise to help capture the essence of the original works.

Jenny Dyson – Flute

Jenny has performed with the BBC Philharmonic, the Hallé, BBC Symphony Orchestra, and Royal Liverpool Philharmonic. As principal flute of the Kaleidoscope Orchestra, Jenny has recorded with artists such as Flux Pavilion, performed for Gatecrasher Classical and Cream Classical Ibiza.

As a soloist, Jenny has performed with orchestras in the UK and abroad, including performances of Malcolm Arnold's 2nd flute concerto and Mozart's Flute and Harp Concerto. Jenny is also making a name for herself in contemporary music, playing at Huddersfield Contemporary Music Festival, the North West Music Festival and BBC Radio 3's Exposure series.

Silvia Lucas – Piano

Silvia Lucas is a Spanish contemporary pianist and electronic performer currently based in Manchester, UK. She is highly in demand and is quickly establishing herself as one of the leading figures in the performance of new works for piano and multimedia.

In 2020, Silvia obtained a PhD from the Royal Northern College of Music (Manchester, UK), where she was also highly commended as a performer in the 2015 Gold Medal Weekend. Ever since, she has enjoyed a very active career, collaborating and premiering a large number of works for piano and electronics, most of these dedicated to her. She has given solo recitals in the United States, Spain, United Kingdom and Germany, and often appears as a solo artist in many contemporary music festivals.

Silvia is also the artistic director and founder of NoiseScenes, a concert series featuring commissions of new electroacoustic music and performance, alongside her own performances of older and newer works.

Dewi Tudor Jones – Violin

Dewi Tudor Jones is a violinist, teacher and composer based in Manchester. He studied Music at The University of Manchester and the Royal Northern College of Music. He now works with orchestras including the Royal Liverpool Philharmonic, Hallé, Opera North and many more as part of a varied freelance career. He teaches and runs ensembles at Loreto Sixth Form College and Yorkshire Young Musicians at Leeds College of Music, and composes music for television and media which is used around the world.

Get the Audio

The audio files for this book are available to download for free from **www.fundamental-changes.com.** The link is in the top right-hand corner. Click on the "Guitar" link then simply select this book title from the drop-down menu and follow the instructions to get the audio.

We recommend that you download the files directly to your computer, not to your tablet, and extract them there before adding them to your media library.

Get the Video

The supporting examples for every piece, selected performances, and clips from my workshops with classical musicians are available on YouTube so you can see the exact technique, fingerings and hand positions I'm using.

Follow the link below or scan the QR code with a smart phone camera to find the Solo Electric Guitar playlist on YouTube:

https://geni.us/rtyt

Join the **Fundamental Changes Guitar Community** on Facebook, where you can ask questions, hear about upcoming books and get feedback on your playing.

Instagram: **FundamentalChanges**

Chapter One – *Syrinx* (Claude Debussy)

Claude Debussy provided a French response to the predominantly Germanic 19th century Romantic movement. He concerned himself with colour and mood, and his sensual, impressionistic approach to music prioritised the expression in each "musical moment", rather than the structure of the whole piece.

He was greatly influenced by East Asian music, such as the Indonesian gamelan music that he witnessed at the Paris World's Fair in 1889, which led him to incorporate pentatonic scales and sustained drones into his style.

Debussy composed this solo flute piece as theatre music in 1913. *Syrinx*'s allusions to nymphs and carnality (with its late-Romantic expressivity) was extremely provocative to an Edwardian audience. Its free time and open form were important developments in classical music, and it is still considered a cornerstone of flute repertoire.

To help interpret Debussy's original intention, I've drawn influence from Jeff Beck and David Gilmour, as well as players who use extensive legato like Allan Holdsworth, who was greatly influenced by the saxophone.

Inspired by Jeff Beck's incredible control over every note, I've played this piece fingerstyle to allow easier muting of any unused strings. As there is nothing to hide behind, eliminating unwanted string noise is a central part of its performance. Listen to Jeff Beck's live performance of *Over the Rainbow* for an example of the subtleties that can be achieved with your fingers.

Most of this piece is played in single notes but occasionally I've allowed several notes to bleed together into close-interval *cluster* chords, to add something distinctively guitar-esque to the original flute melody. Conversely, I've used bending and the whammy bar to interpret the flute's pitch inflections.

You'll notice the scary-looking rhythms but listen to my audio recording and the original flute version to help you learn each phrase.

Let-Ring Scales

There are several places in this piece where notes from the melody are allowed to sustain into each other. This is easy enough if the melody happens to be the notes of a chord, but if the melody is moving stepwise in intervals of major or minor 2nds then careful fingering choices are needed to unlock these beautiful, characterful close-interval sounds.

Letting notes ring together like this is reminiscent of a harp or kora, and Country guitar players cleverly arrange their licks to include open strings to achieve a similar effect. (For example, *Jerry's Breakdown* by Jerry Reed & Chet Atkins, where the step-wise melody is arranged one-note-per-string).

Depending on the key of the piece, open strings might be available to help out, as in this example showing an ascending A Minor Pentatonic scale.

Example 1a:

Check out the supporting video clips to see these exercises performed.

Wide stretches are needed when open strings aren't available, so this approach is usually limited to higher frets where the spacing is closer.

Here, the A Natural Minor scale is broken up into descending three-note clusters. Keep the thumb very low on the back of the neck and tilt the guitar neck upwards to help with the wide stretches. Picking close to the bridge adds a pleasingly un-guitaristic tone associated with the cimbalom/kalimba/koto.

Example 1b:

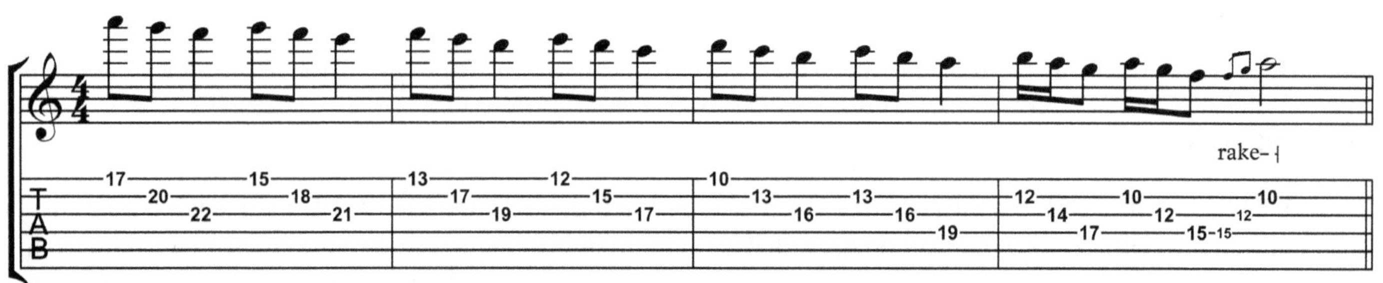

Using the Whammy Bar

The whammy bar is an important addition to our palette of expressive techniques, and lets us bend notes in unexpected ways to mimic the dips and swoops of woodwind instruments.

You can use the bar to "scoop" up into a target note by depressing it before plucking the note. Once the note is ringing, the bar is then repeatedly "dipped" to add rhythmic pulses to a held note.

I suggest cradling the bar in the second to fourth fingers while holding the pick in the first finger. If you're not using a pick then this grip still gives you the freedom to either pluck with the thumb for a soft tone, or make a "pretend pick" with your first finger and thumb (*à la* Jeff Beck) for a sharper attack.

Example 1c:

The next example is best performed on a Floyd Rose or floating bridge guitar, or a standard Fender Strat bridge that is set up to float.

The bar is used to raise the pitch before the note and release down onto it (the opposite of Example 1c). You can perform this with the bar in the standard position by pulling the cupped picking hand away from the guitar as you pick, or by spinning the bar 180° away from the neck and quickly pressing down as you hammer onto the notes with the fretting hand without picking.

Jason Becker uses this approach at the end of his piece *Altitudes.* This articulation has an more exotic quality, thanks to the dissonant and unexpected approach to each note from above. As far as I know, there's no accepted term for this inverted scoop, so I humbly suggest the onomatopoeic "yoing" is universally adopted!

Example 1d:

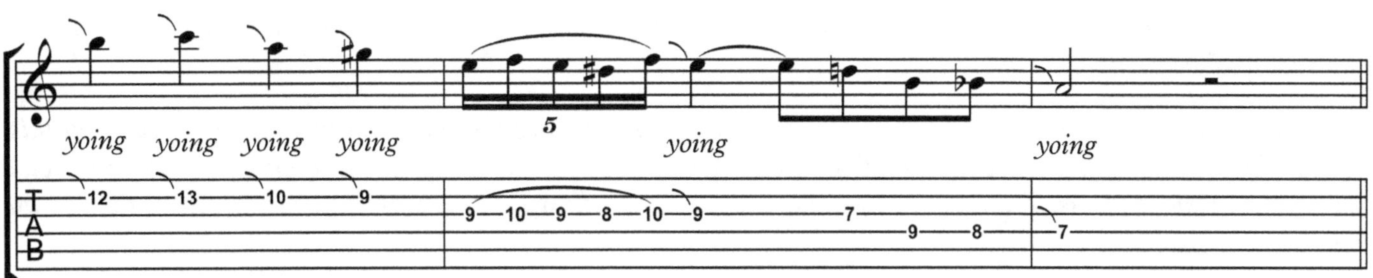

It was fascinating to find that each of the musicians I talked to had contrasting views on interpretation and the role of both the score and recordings. Jenny's advice for learning a new piece of music is to balance score-analysis with seeking inspiration from other flautists' interpretations.

Interview with flautist Jenny Dyson

JD: "Look through the score; look for the shapes and phrases and read it along to a variety of recordings. This process can help you to identify bits of the piece that strike a chord with you, or conversely don't match your taste. Form your own opinions. Either positive or negative reactions are great and will help you build your own interpretation later on."

When thinking about what expression to put into the piece, Jenny was quick to highlight *Syrinx's* theatrical origin:

JD: "There's a lot of context and before we even start playing the notes we have to put ourselves into the scene. [The scene is Pan's Cave, and he is playing the flute as he is close to death]. *You also have to take into consideration the story of Pan's flute. Syrinx is the name of his flute, or Pan-pipes, and it's named after a nymph he pursued."*

The nymph hid and transformed herself to become water reeds. When Pan couldn't find her, he angrily cut down all the reeds and, upon realising that he'd killed the nymph with whom he was in love, made a flute from those reeds. Keep this story is mind when listening to the piece.

Jenny enthused about the importance of rhythm in general.

JD: "This is a very free piece, but make sure your rhythm is 'correct' at first. The rhythm is so powerful, it's the movement of the music. Debussy uses rhythm in a very prescriptive way, and here it's used to ramp up tension.

There are moments of absolute rapture and other moments of desperation, and it flips very quickly between the two, making for quite an emotionally volatile landscape."

Jenny's copy of the score includes lines of dialogue as they would be spoken between the musical phrases and she likes to read these in her head during a performance to help space out the music.

JD: "It should have space, so it really feels improvisatory ... When translating from flute to electric guitar, especially in this genre of music, you want to make sure there aren't any sharp edges. Every [note] *should have a rounded edge. There's no staccatissimo or moments when it cuts off abruptly, so do anything you can to let the sound disperse into the air."*

"Think about taking breaths [to link phrases together]. *I'm playing the flute, but when you're learning this, sing it through, and sing as you're playing* [the guitar]. *Singing, and needing to breathe, will let you decide where the musical phrases start and stop. Think about how you would make this sound. Then try to recreate that on your instrument."*

Playing Notes:

Bars 1-2: Variations on this opening motif are repeated a few times throughout the piece. Keep the fretting hand square-on to the fretboard, with the thumb low on the back of the neck to maximise your stretch and finger independence. It's important to make the line as legato as possible, so tapping maximises the number of notes on each string while avoiding awkward, noisy position-shifts. The unconventional fingering at the end of bar one into bar two also helps us move back up the fretboard. Tapping the 20th fret then gives the fretting hand time to reposition for the 19th fret.

Bars 5-6: Several different techniques are combined here to reproduce the necessary notes. The arpeggio notes in bar five should ring together like a spread piano chord. The high Ab is an artificial harmonic, played by fretting the 18th fret, then touching the string with the picking hand where an imaginary 30th fret would be.

A classical guitarist would play artificial harmonics by pointing the first finger at the harmonic node and plucking with the thumb. However, it is better for us to adopt the bass guitar method and touch the node with the side of the thumb and pluck with a finger. This should be practiced in isolation to get a clear sound.

Bar 7: Feedback relies on a certain amount of gain and volume, so this aspect will not be possible if practicing quietly. When performing, it's crucial to check beforehand whether your setup will feed back. Artists who use intentional feedback creatively, including the late Gary Moore, often mark the stage with tape to show where they should stand to get perfect feedback.

Bar 11-12: It can be tricky to get the rhythm of the grace notes correct during the already fast legato passage. Just be sure to slow-down the whole phrase to practice evenly, and listen to the demo recording as well as other performances by flautists to hear how this line can be phrased.

Bar 13: More rhythmic fun here! As with the rest of this piece, the intricate rhythms can be indicative rather than exact. Each of these descending chromatic lines should sustain the tapped note then rush through the three pull-offs to land with emphasis on the next string. Imagine the melody overflowing in bursts onto each new string.

Bar 15: Practice bending the string down a semitone by fretting the 6th note, then using the bar to dip the 7th fret to the same pitch. Once you are comfortable with how much pressure this takes and the sound of the interval, you'll be able to do it in context. If you don't have a whammy bar, then grace note pull-offs, or experimenting with pre-bends from the 6th fret are excellent substitutes.

Bar 18: Here, a new chordal texture is introduced. The melody forms an F# minor chord which is held down and allowed to sustain. With a moderately overdriven tone, this will give the chord a crunchy sound, emphasising the crescendo.

JD: "Pan was a sick character mentally. He might be looking back at his life, and there are times when the sun comes out and it's bathed in warmth [bars 19-20] *but then it transforms really quickly and interestingly to something darker* [continuing to bar 24]. *"*

Bar 21: Another nice little chordal moment, but this time the cluster of close intervals means a tapped note is easiest. Give the picking hand time to reposition by hammering onto the 12th fret of the B string.

Bar 22: The tapped D note (10th fret) might seem unnecessary, but following the fingering keeps the line fluid and smooth. The fretting hand stretches out more towards the end of the phrase, so keep the thumb low on the back and point the guitar skywards (guitar hero pose #3) to make it less of a strain.

Bar 23-24: Fret the 9th fret with the third finger – this way the first finger lays flat and mutes adjacent strings behind it, allowing you to be much more gung-ho when trilling with the tapped notes.

Bar 26-30: This material should feel quite familiar by now but pay attention to the fingerings. When a melody repeats, think about how you could play it differently – maybe with different dynamics, tempo, or by adjusting your tone with a pickup change or the position of the pick.

Bar 31 to End: Bending a note with the whammy bar can leave your picking hand in quite a compromising position. The best way to finish the piece cleanly would be with a volume pedal, or by carefully release the fretting hand pressure. You don't want to let the bar return to pitch with the note still sounding.

JD: "I think [bar 33] *is a key moment. We get Bb throughout the piece, but it's only at the end that we get this B natural, and there's something really odd about it. Think about this being* [Pan's] *last, laboured breath. The re-articulation of the last Eb is important. It's like his last heartbeat."*

Syrinx – C. Debussy

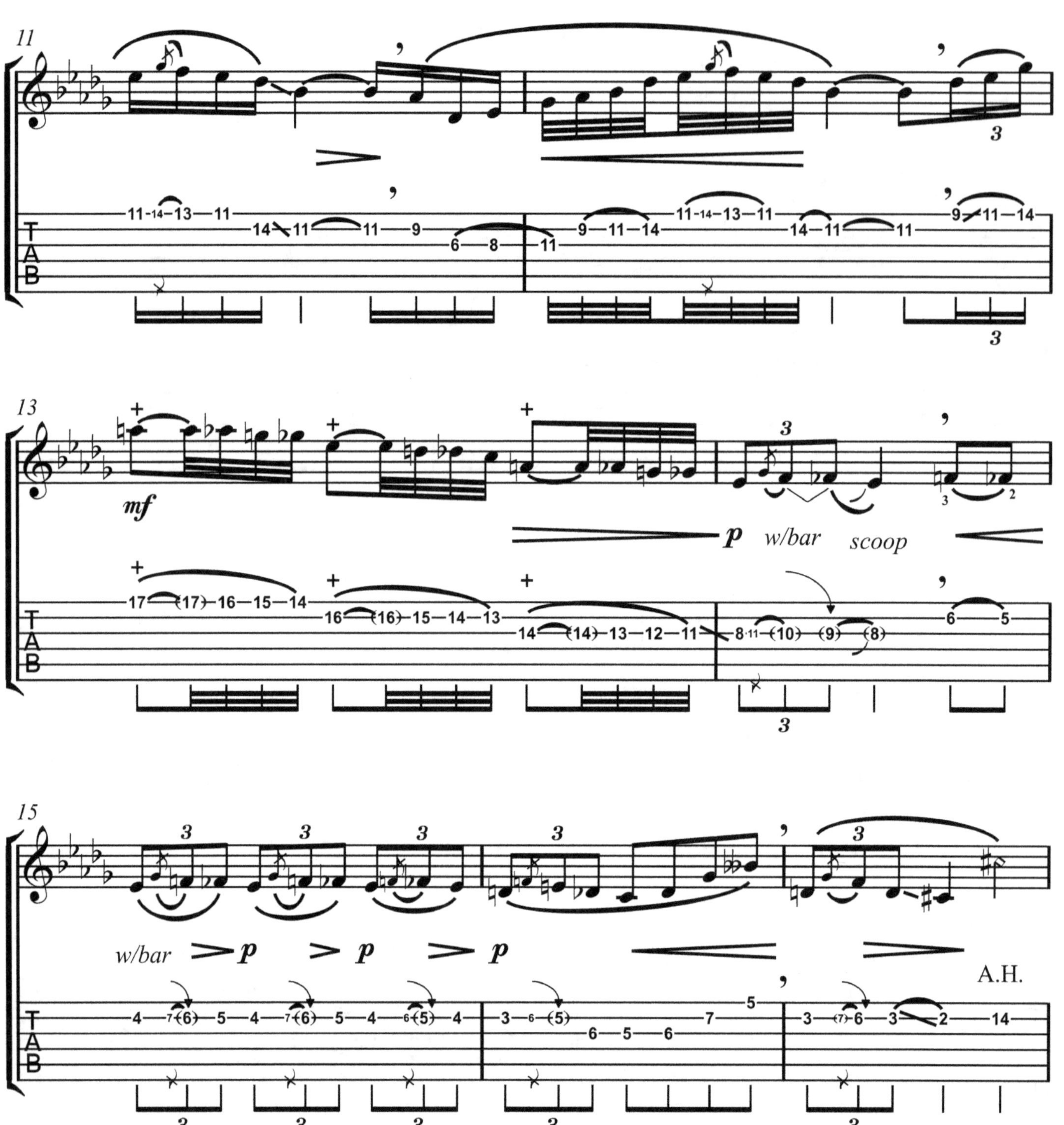
11
13
mf
p
w/bar
scoop
15
w/bar
p
p
p
A.H.

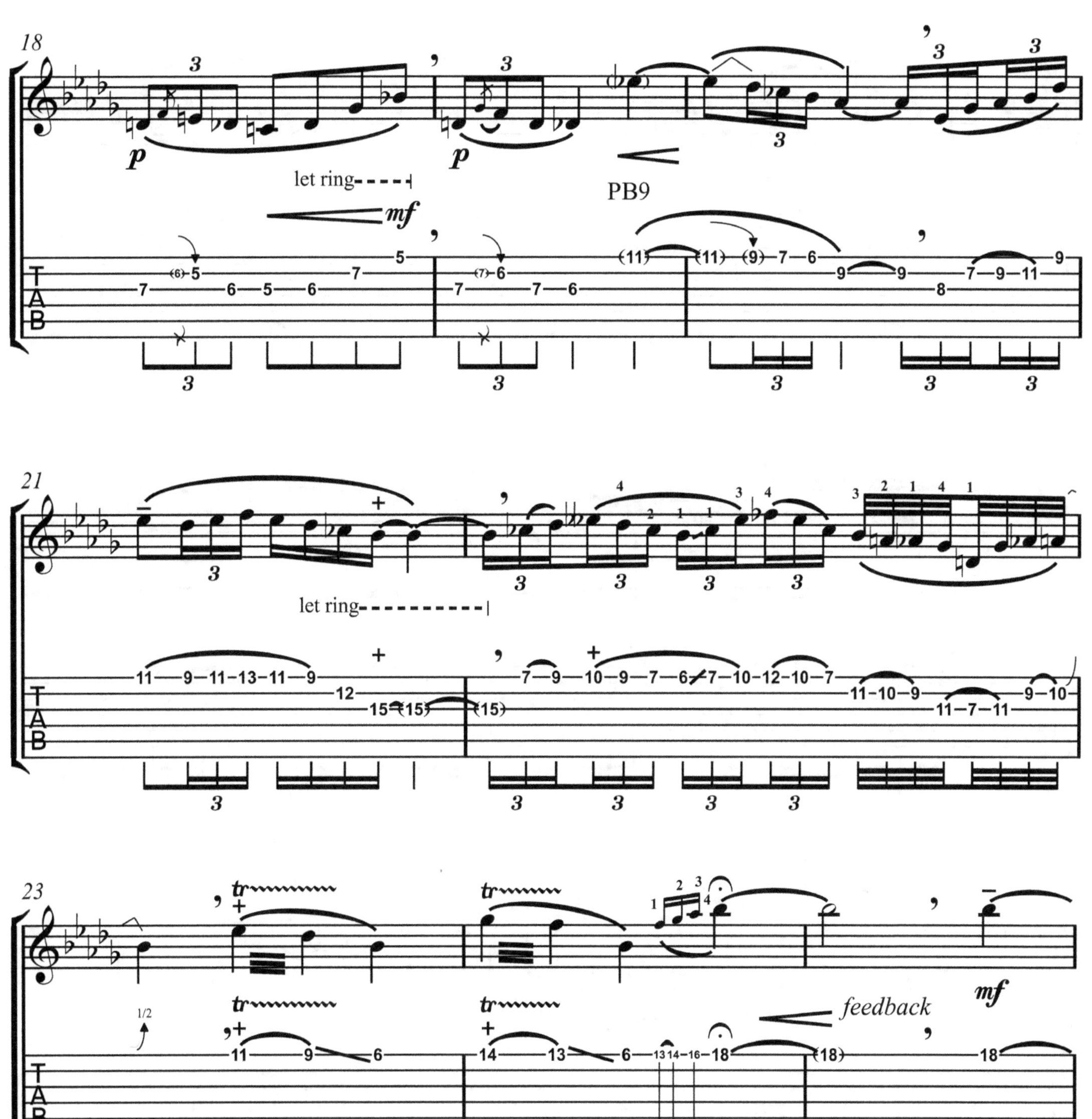

let ring
mf
PB9
let ring
feedback
mf

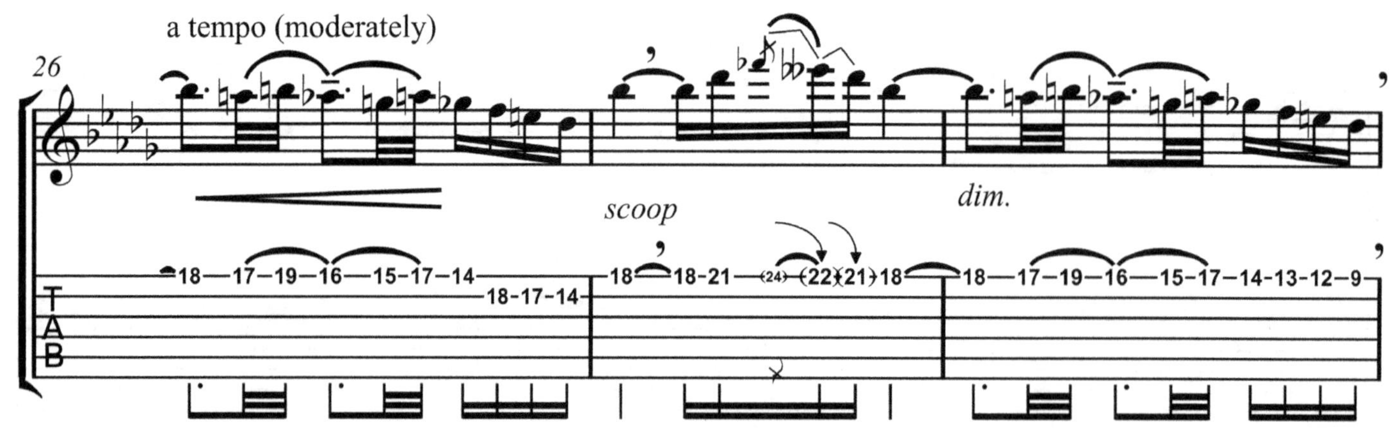
a tempo (moderately)
26
scoop
dim.

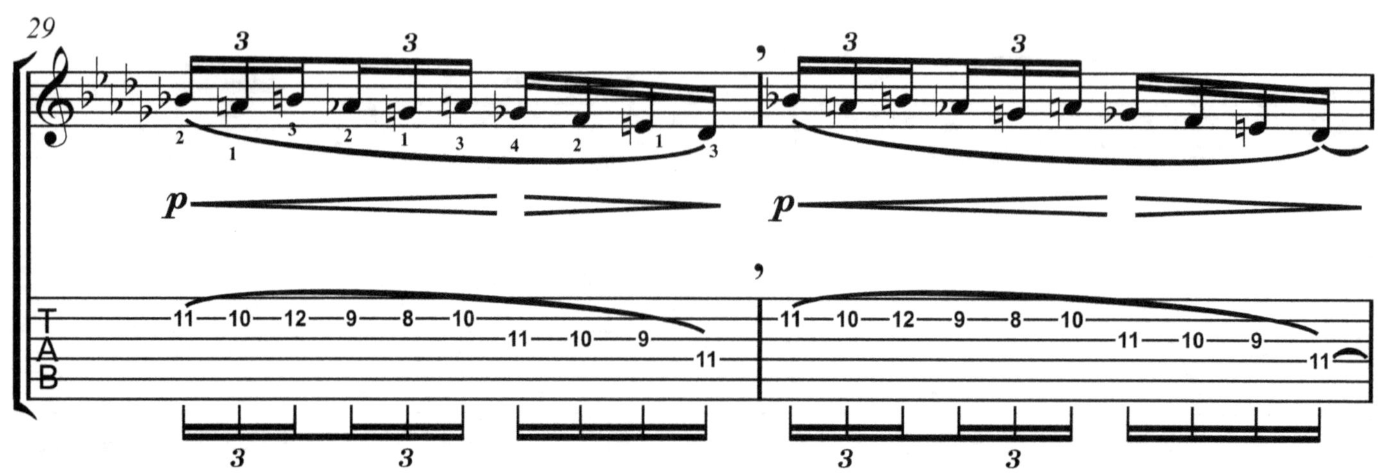
29

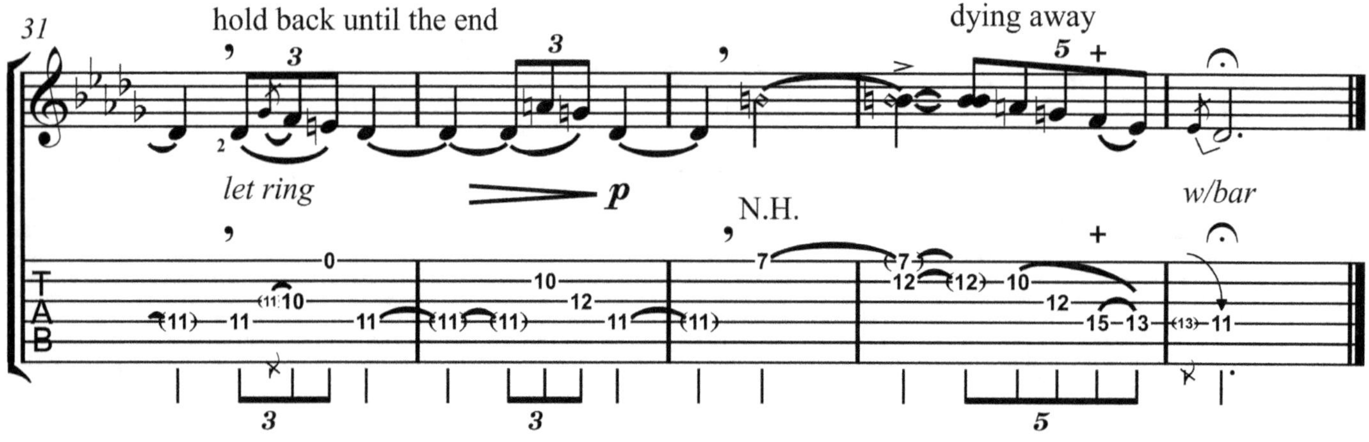
31
hold back until the end
dying away
let ring
N.H.
w/bar

Chapter Two – *Prelude No. 16, Opus 28* (Frédéric Chopin)

Frédéric Chopin (1810-1849), the Polish pianist and composer, was a key figure in the Romantic period of classical music (roughly speaking, the 19th century). His music is typically Romantic, featuring virtuosic playing, emotive imagery, dramatic dynamic contrasts, and chromatic harmony that doesn't resolve quite as predictably as the earlier Classical or Baroque styles.

The piano was a key development in this regard. Its new iron frame allowed for high-tension metal strings, which largely replaced the earlier harpsichords that had animal-gut strings. A harpsichord plucks every note at the same volume, while the piano hammers the string with varying strength, depending on the player's attack. The new pianoforte (literally *quiet-loud* in Italian) became all the rage because of the new dimensions that its dynamics added to keyboard music.

Chopin wrote almost exclusively for solo piano, producing many collections of etudes, preludes, nocturnes and various European folk dances. His pieces are still widely enjoyed and central to the instrument's repertoire.

To successfully perform piano music on guitar one needs to reduce the note-density and make careful fingering choices. In essence, I've transcribed the right-hand melody from the original prelude and simply omitted the chords. This prelude is packed with great chord-tone phrases that spell out the underlying harmony, meaning that the melody still gives us a sense of the chord progression.

The chord symbols above the stave will help you to analyse the composition or create a duet performance. Knowing the underlying harmony will also help you to extract phrases to apply in your rock soloing.

The low E string is tuned down to D, and the piece is transposed from Bb Minor down three frets to G Minor. This allows the piece to fit the range of a standard 22-fret electric guitar.

Dynamics

Romantic piano music was all about expressive, loud-quiet contrasts, which you should incorporate on guitar. However, maintaining enough control to pick evenly while changing how hard you dig into the strings will take practice.

In certain bars I used an octave/pitch shifter effect (KMA Moai Maea) set to -1 octave, mixed quieter than the dry signal to thicken and support where indicated. This imitates the moments when the original piano piece plays the same notes in both hands.

Chromatic Approach to Arpeggios

Approaching the notes of a chord from one fret above or below is a common melodic approach in classical music, jazz, and metal. Players as diverse as Django Reinhardt and Randy Rhoads have made use of this technique.

The example below features pairs of semitones which outline a D major chord (chord V in G Minor). Play the second of each pair on its own and you should recognise the familiar A-shape barre chord. The first bar shows the D arpeggio on its own, then each chord tone is approached from a semitone below, then above.

Example 2a:

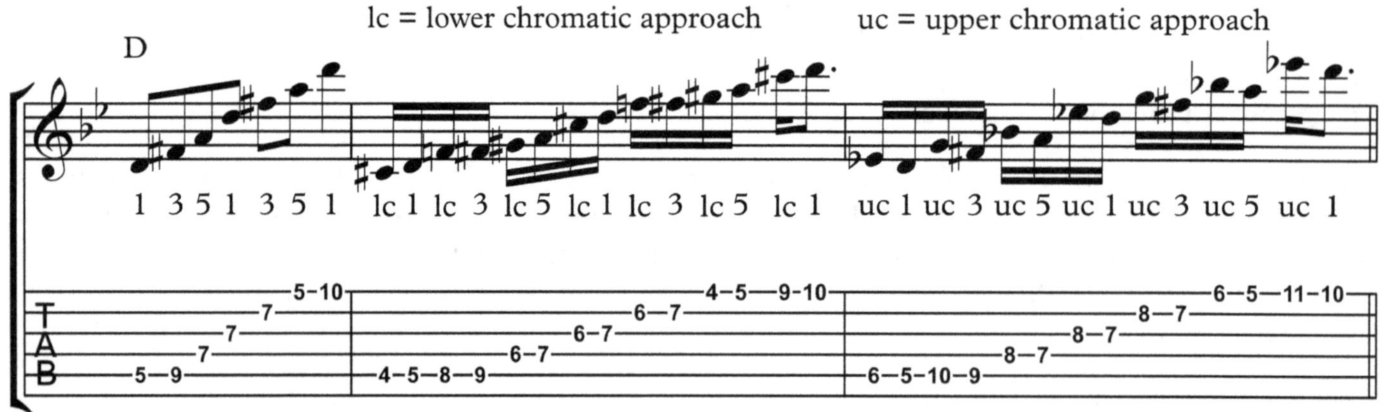

After working through arpeggio shapes with these chromatic approach notes, you'll be able to visualise them more easily. Here's a classically tinged metal lick that adapts the end of Chopin's prelude.

Example 2b:

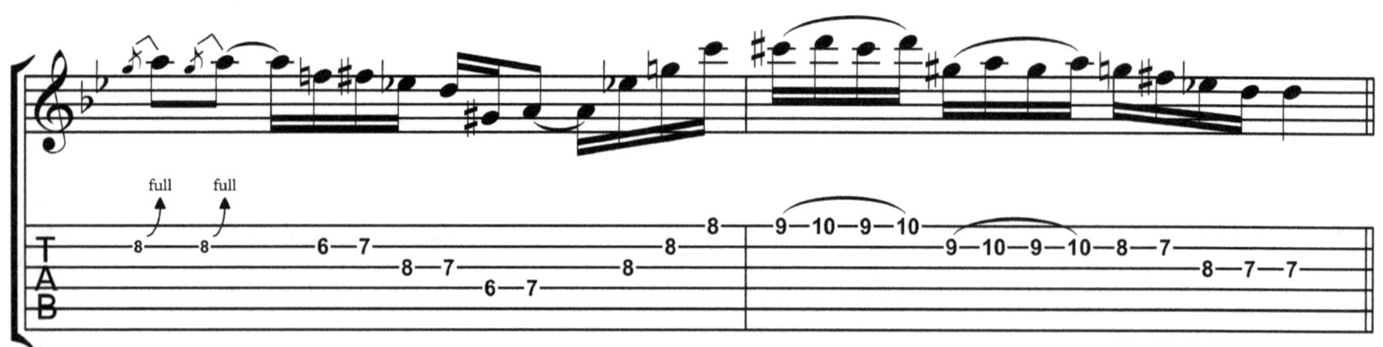

Interview with Silvia Lucas:

I asked Silvia how she would embark on learning a new piece. She was very clear that she would start with the sheet music and first observe all the instructions it contains before making any artistic decisions.

SL: "When you look at a score, there's all your instructions and it's quite definite. When I'm learning a piece, I start from the text.

I follow the score 100%, and turn that into sound. I learn everything, I rationalise everything I see in the score, and then my performance is my way of forgetting what I've learned. It's very important to understand what the parameters are, and how they sound. Then, in a way, my performance is about what I disregard, or how I make it more humane."

There's no single correct approach and it's interesting that Silvia contrasts Jenny in arguing against listening to other performers early on.

SL: "I don't listen to pieces as part of my learning process; perhaps I don't want to taint my own interpretation ... It could influence my decisions if I listen to others early on. [When I have listened to a recording] *I've not considered the phrasing of the musical ideas, it's not come from me ... just copy aurally rather than by thinking about it."*

Silvia also highlighted how developing a good technique early on gives you the freedom to be creative later.

SL: "There'll be some points in the learning process where it's going to be metronomic and unmusical, but it's in the service of musicianship at a later stage. This will give me a cleaner canvas to put colour on, when my playing is very even.

I would prepare differently for a recording session or a live performance. For a live performance there are things I would disregard more. If you were playing in a big hall with lots of reverb, for example, you might need to change certain rhythms.

I would take the metronome approach for quite some time, make sure that all the figures – whether scales, intervallic licks or chromatics – sound the same. Good piano technique basically means that you don't have any unwanted accents, the notes are all the same length, and crescendos are even and consistent.

Be methodical. I'll have my blank canvas, then I'm going to do the outlines, then I'll start blurring them and putting colour in ... So here [in the score], *this means I'm going to get all the semiquavers even, get rid of unwanted accents. If I want an accent, I'll put it in later, but it shouldn't be an accident of my technique."*

This is great advice. Unlearning mistakes and technical shortcomings later will slow down your learning overall. Having the patience to iron-out imperfections early on will pay dividends, both in creative control and time saved.

SL: "Don't add expression too early or you'll still be fixing holes while trying to put colour in."

Lastly, Silvia points out the essence that this Prelude is trying to convey. It is a muscular, technical show-piece that benefits from bold confident performance.

SL: "Chopin was around a little later than Liszt and Paganini, but was still in the age of the virtuoso performer. It is, after all, a show-off piece, so take the 'rockstar' mindset but develop it with the principles of control and expression."

However, as with shred guitar, technical fireworks work best in service of something bigger. While pure speed might wow other customers at the local guitar shop, it's more important to make sure the melody and harmony are still discernible.

SL: "Some people play this piece disgustingly fast! Chopin wouldn't put metronome marks on his scores, but Presto con Fuoco means fast with fire. That said, the audience can't understand what's being said if it's too fast, and the novelty of looking at the fast fingers will wear off very quickly"

Playing Notes:

Tuning: Drop-D tuning

Bar 1: Playing the tritone with fingers 2 and 3 in the opening chords means you can hold them down throughout, and use fingers 4 and 1 to play the descending melody. Rake the pick slowly across each of these chords then have a short pause at the end. They are the calm inhale before the ensuing musical rollercoaster!

Bar 2: Chopin marked his original to be played *presto con fuoco*. "Presto" equates to 168-200 bpm and *con fuoco* means "with fire". My demo is slower at 120-140bpm, which is quite ambitious enough.

Bar 3: The fingering for the notes on the high E string may seem puzzling. When practicing this piece, I was making unwanted string noise before developing this fingering. Hammering on with the second finger frees the first finger to mute the B and G strings. After tapping the high notes, the fretting hand can return to the more typical 1-2-4 fingering pattern.

SL: "The technical limitations of the guitar become quite apparent here. The higher you go, it gets quieter and has less sustain, but Chopin notates the opposite, to crescendo on the highest notes."

You could just pile on more distortion to counteract this shortcoming, but a compressor and a volume pedal won't generate quite as much unwanted noise.

Bar 5: Joe Satriani fans will find this bar quite easy, but don't let the legato make your timing suffer.

Bar 6: Use fretting hand tapping to play the descending notes, one on each string. This is much more fluid than picking, but be careful that you don't let them ring together as a chord. Flatten the fingers slightly across the strings and tap with the pad of each finger to mute the previous string as it come down.

Bar 8: Hybrid picking is a great way of quickly alternating between non-adjacent strings. The notes on the E string are plucked with the second finger, while all the rest are downstrokes with the pick. Break down this line into three-note fragments, repeating each three-note group in isolation. Gradually connect them together once the picking pattern starts to feel natural.

SL: "I might try to get the polyphony out of [bars 8-9] *because it's counterpoint, if you want to think of it that way. Separate the high and low lines, and give them different tones."*

Bar 10-11: These two bars look and feel very similar to play, but be sure to check through the tab for one different note on the G string.

SL: "The pick accents get in the way of the legato phrasing here and break the flow."

It's good practice to soften your pick-strokes and aim for as little difference between legato and picked notes. It's also possible to hammer on or pull off with extra force to produce accents on the beats without picking.

Bar 24-28: The shape of these bars is as uniform as possible. The consistent picking pattern and legato helps the section to sound fluid, as well as making each bar easier to learn.

Bar 28-31: These bars feature descending phrases that stretch across the beats, contrasted with regular chord changes on each beat. As this is a solo arrangement, it's important to accent the notes on each beat to maintain some impression of the pulse.

Bar 30-31: The original piano piece featured both hands playing in unison starting on beat 4 of bar 30. To emulate this, I engaged an octave pedal set to one octave below, just for five beats.

Bar 32: After the cascade of different rhythmic groupings in bars 28-31, the straight pulse returns. It seemed appropriate to alternate pick this almost riff-like section. See the introductory comments on picking dynamics to give this section character. If fast alternate picking really isn't your forte, then experiment with palm muting while playing legato to get a similarly percussive separation to each note.

Bar 38: A small adjustment was needed here to keep within the guitar's range. The first two notes of bar 38 should be C and D. After trying several options, holding the D for an 1/8th note sounded best. Guitarists with a seven-string instrument are free to put the low C back in on the 7th string. As with bar 30, the piano part plays both hands in unison from here until the end, so I re-engaged the sub-octave pedal.

Bar 38-41: This type of pattern is common in gypsy jazz and is best fingered with fingers 1 and 2, much like Django Reinhardt would have done. It means more lurching around the neck but is easier to visualise and apply in your playing. Start by alternate picking all the notes, then introduce more legato and reduce the palm muting during bar 40.

Bar: 41-42: The huge jump from the 22nd fret down to the 3rd can be risky. Practice playing the first half of bar 41 without looking at the fretboard. Once you have confidence in your accuracy, look ahead to the 3rd fret to make the leap down the neck as quick and accurate as possible.

These last two chords are a breeze compared to the rest of the piece but don't under-sell them! Although they're both marked staccato in the original, I chose to hold the final G minor on longer, raking the strings very close to the bridge to get a zither-like sound, then added some gentle whammy bar vibrato.

Roll off the volume control to clean up your overdriven tone and stop the chord from sounding muddy. This is best done quickly in the rest after the D7 chord.

As a final note, after completing my arrangement independently, I discovered Ron Thal's (aka Bumblefoot) transcription of Chopin's *Fantasie-impromptu in C# Minor*, which uses several similar techniques. Check out archive footage of him performing it online.

Chopin left us with a wealth of solo piano pieces, so maybe have a go at arranging one for yourself. The process will teach you a lot about the layout of the fretboard through finding new ways to locate combinations of notes on the neck.

Prelude No. 16, Op. 28 – F. Chopin

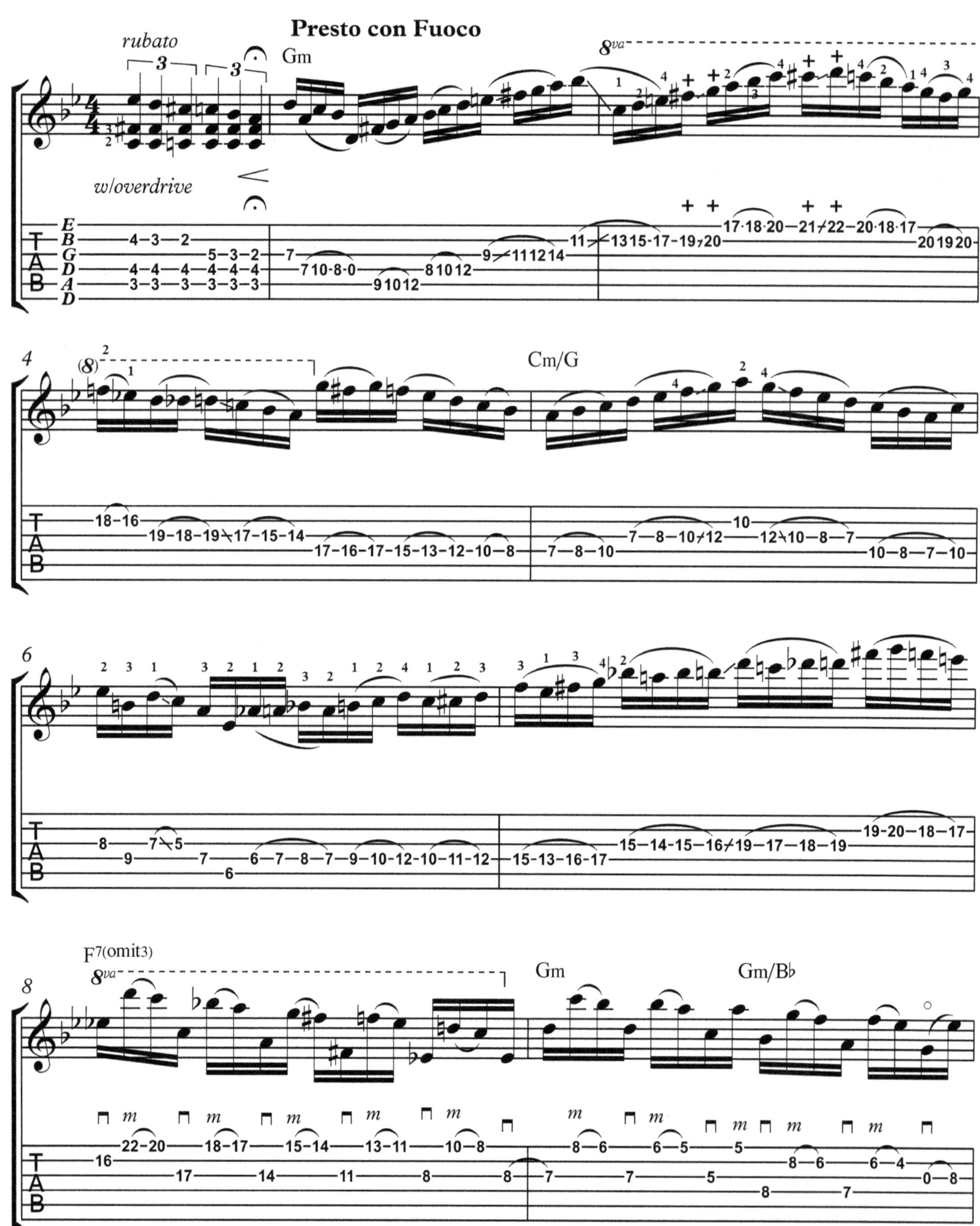

10
F7/C
Gm/B♭
D°
Am/C
12
B♭/D
E♭°
B♭/D
C♯°7
14
C°7
Gm/B♭
D7
16
Gm
8va

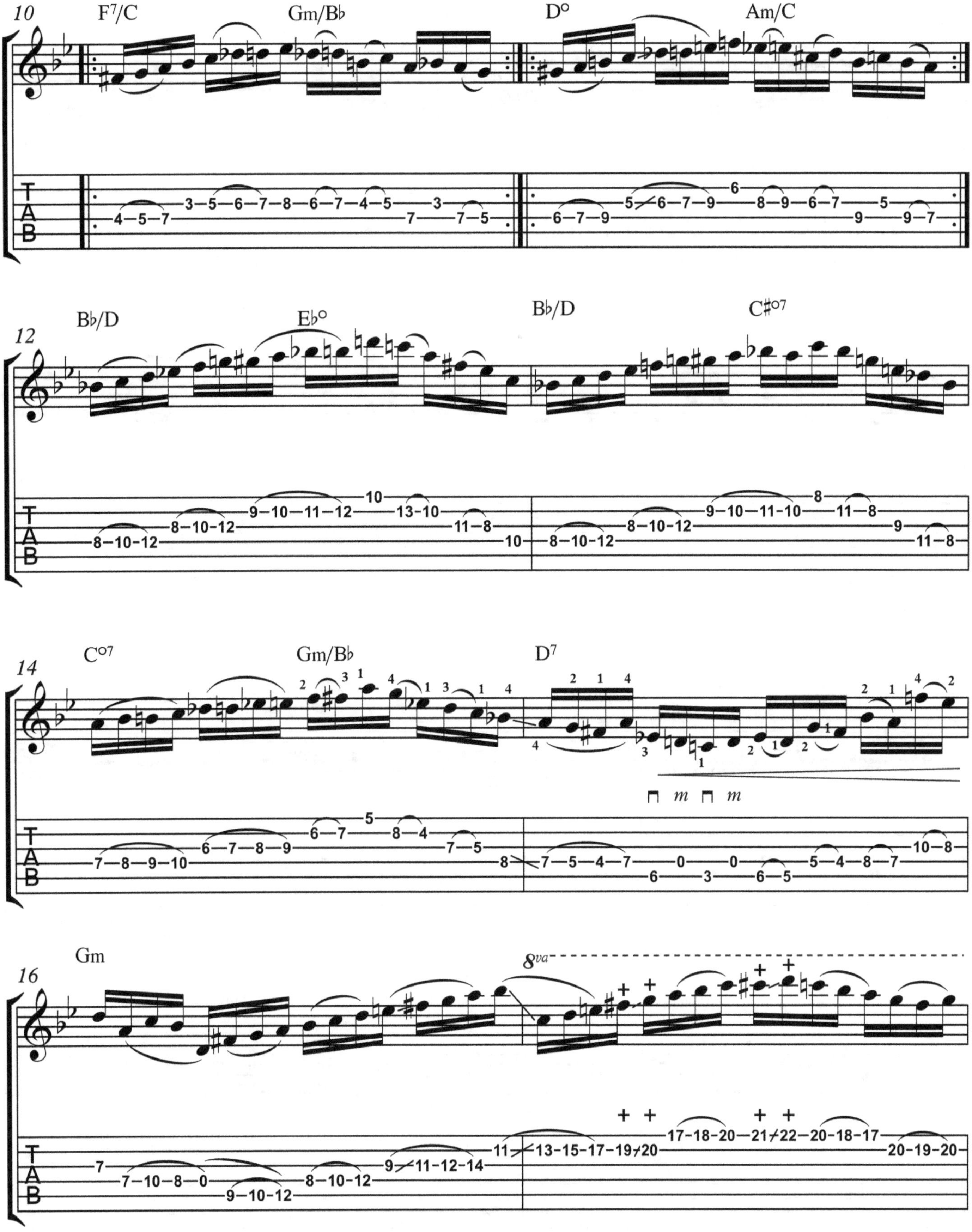

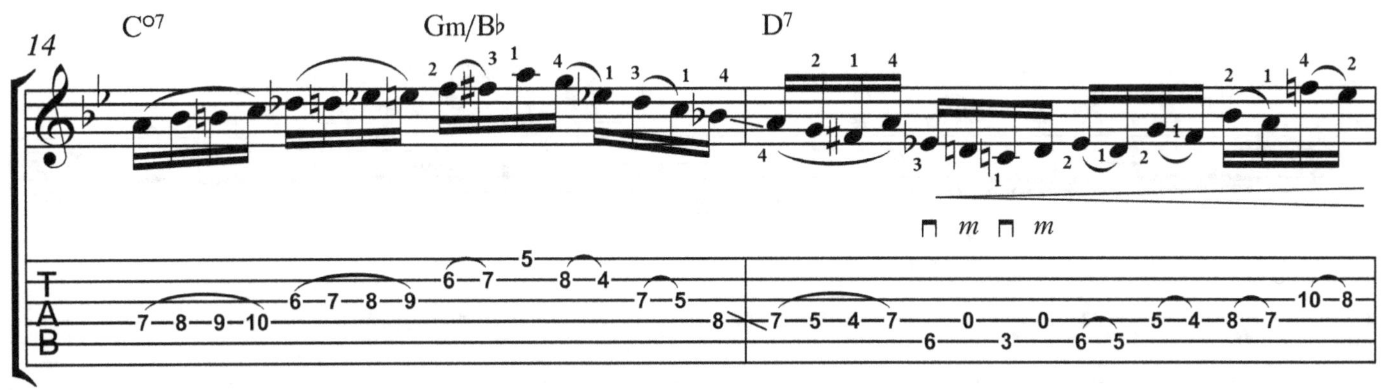

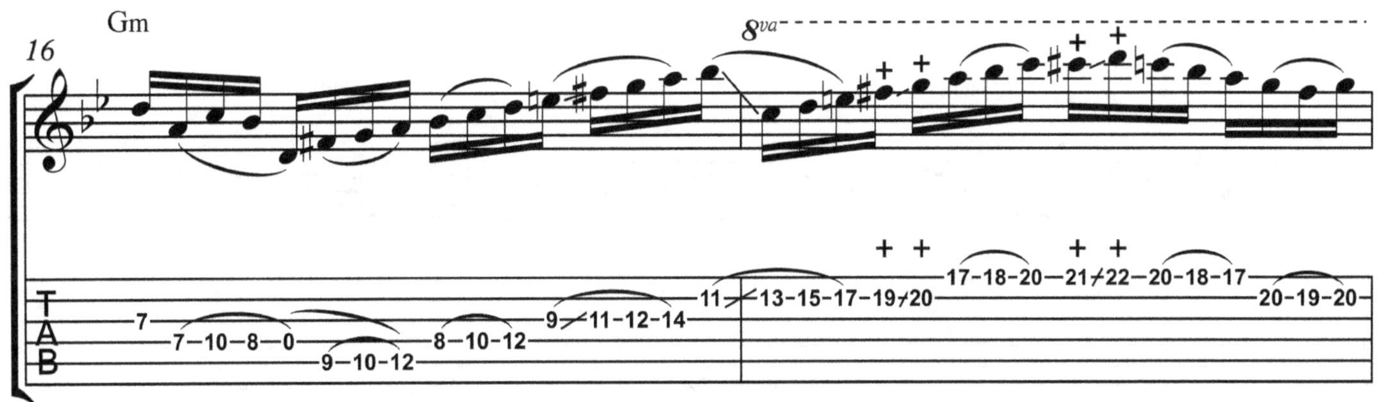

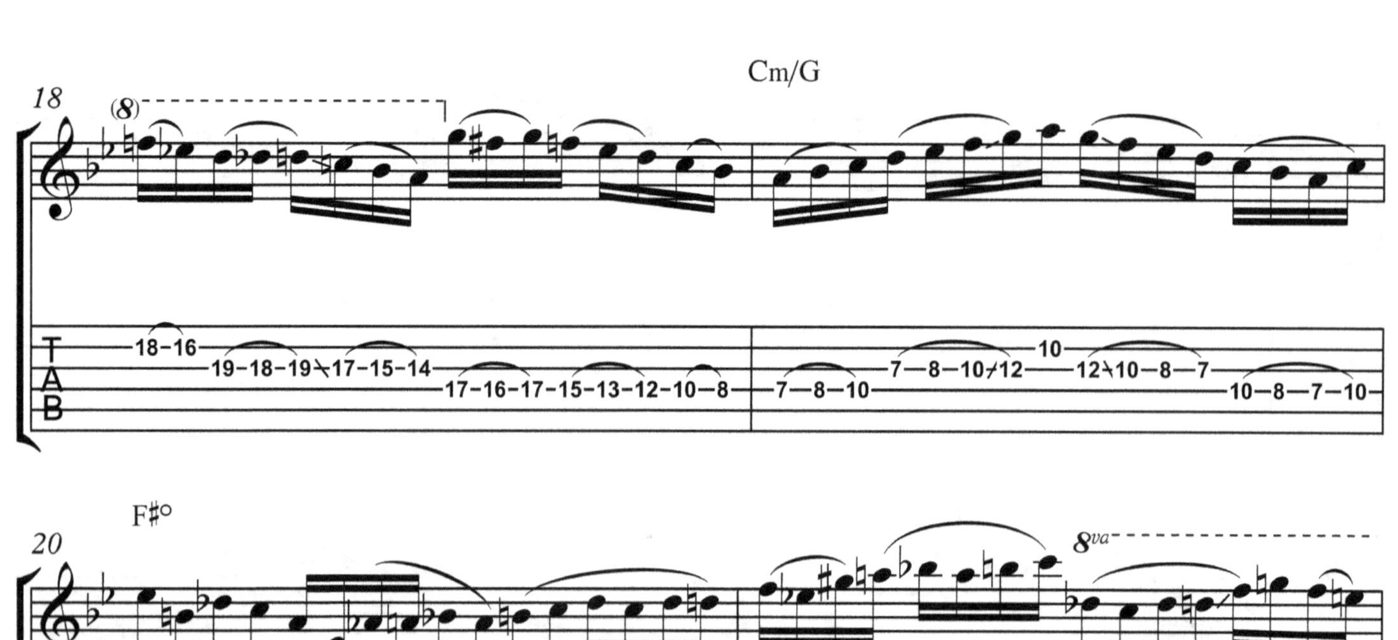
18
Cm/G

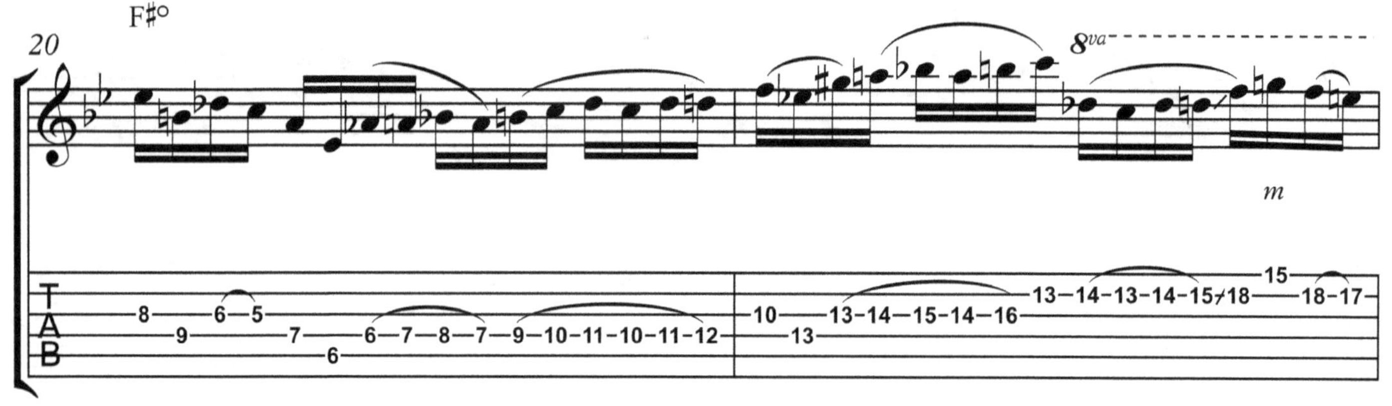
20
F♯°
8va

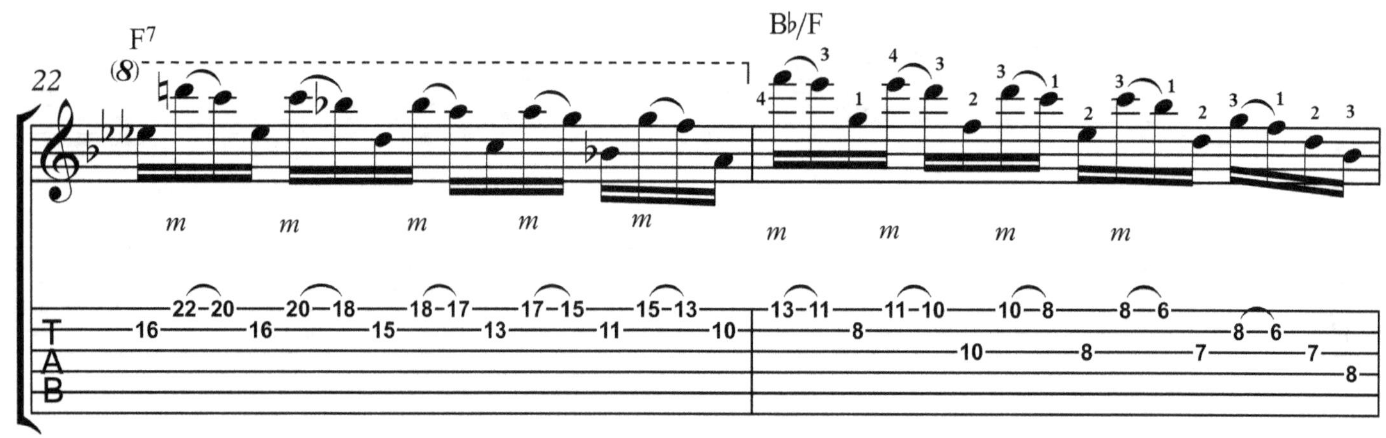
22
F7
B♭/F

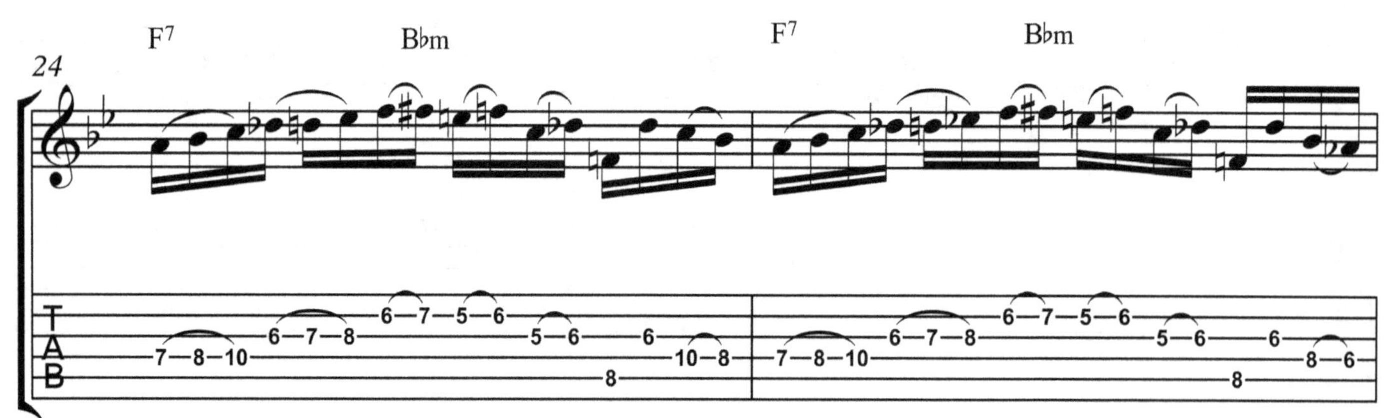
24
F7
B♭m
F7
B♭m

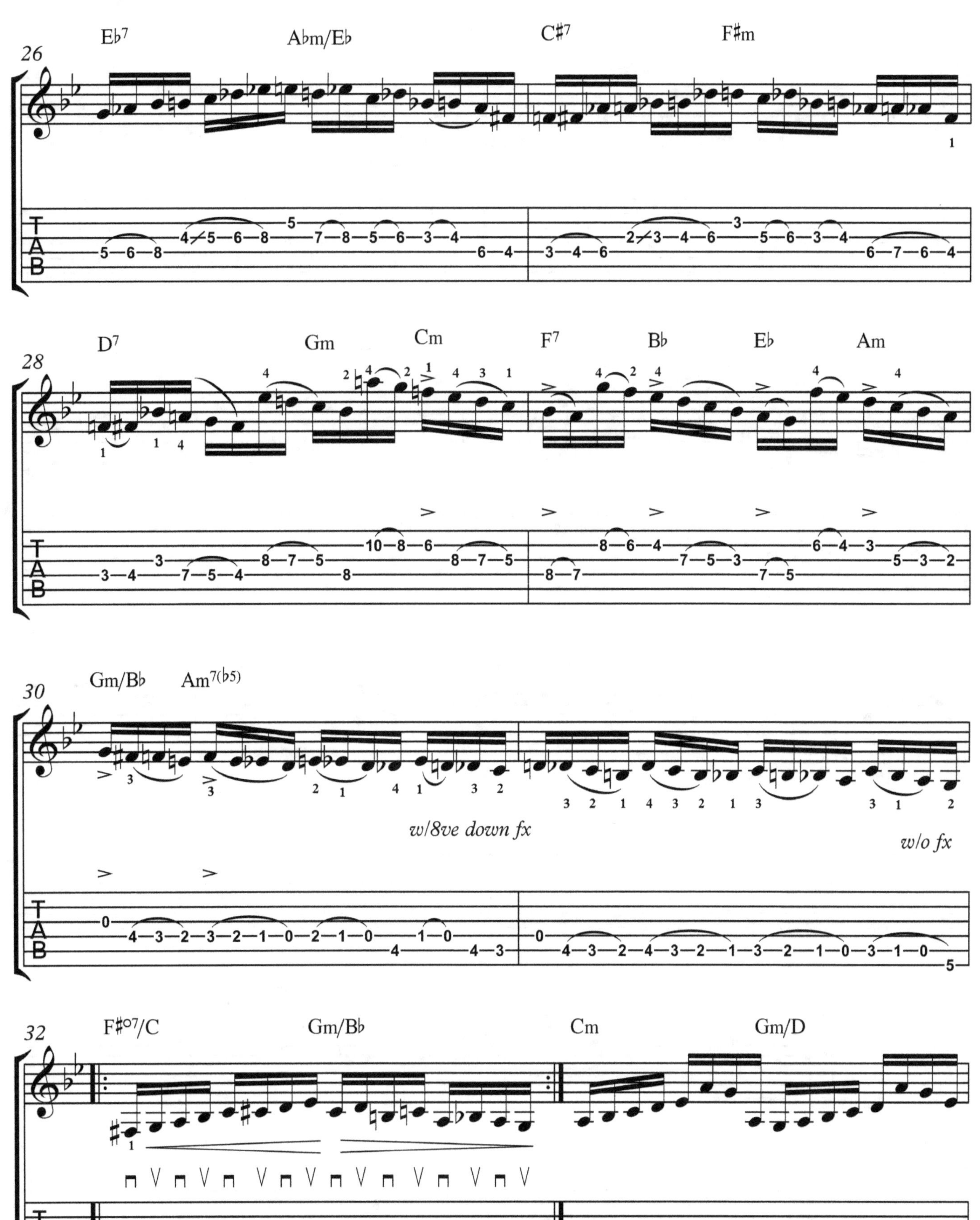
26
E♭7
A♭m/E♭
C♯7
F♯m
28
D7
Gm
Cm
F7
B♭
E♭
Am
30
Gm/B♭
Am7(♭5)
w/8ve down fx
w/o fx
32
F♯o7/C
Gm/B♭
Cm
Gm/D

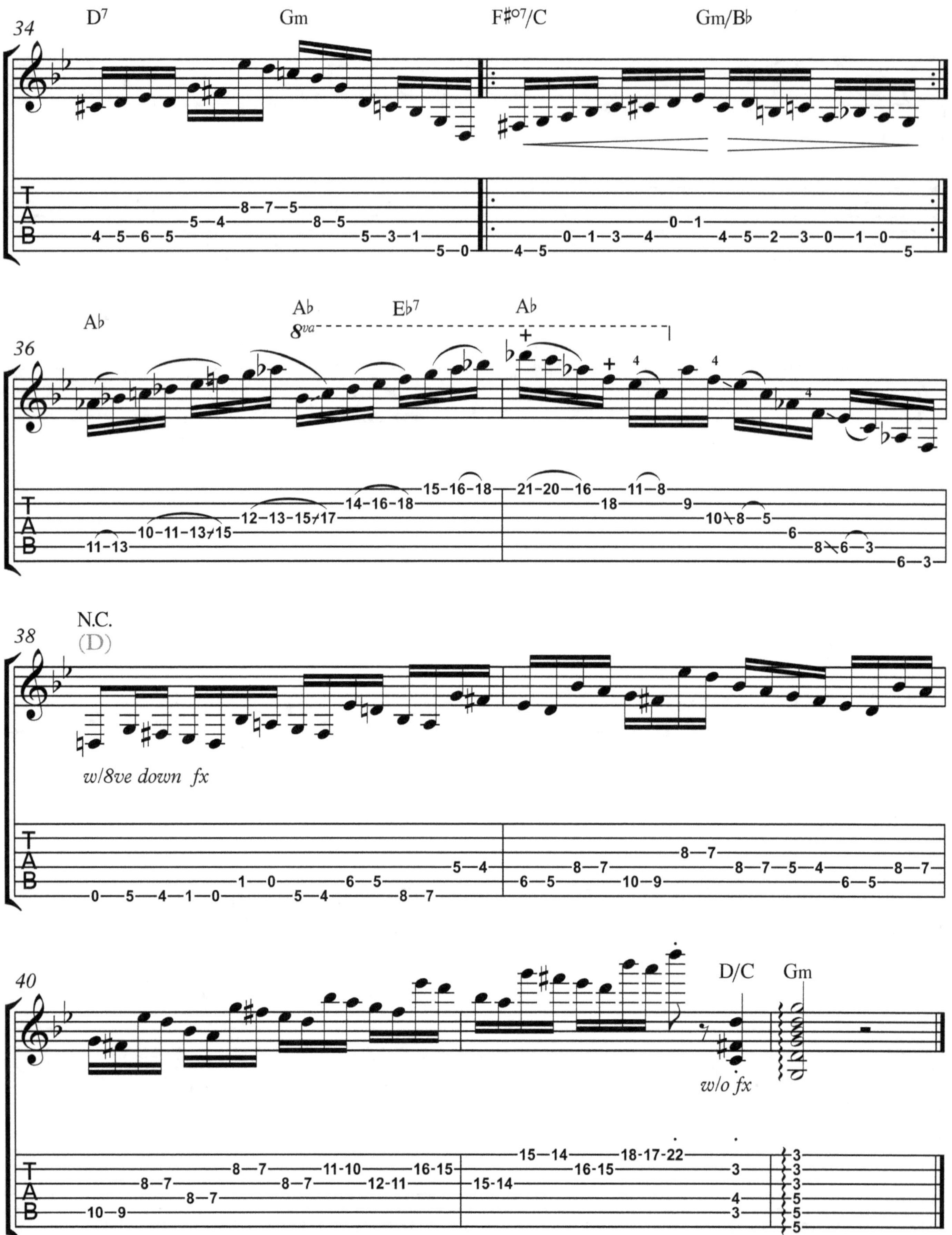
34
D7
Gm
F♯°7/C
Gm/B♭
36
A♭
A♭
8va
E♭7
A♭
38
N.C.
(D)
w/8ve down fx
40
D/C
Gm
w/o fx

Chapter Three – *Violin Partita No. 1 in B Minor (III. Courante)* (J.S. Bach)

The next two pieces come from J.S. Bach's *Partita No. 1 in B Minor* for solo violin. Partitas were a suite of short pieces to be performed together, usually based on dance styles of the time. The B Minor partita has four dances, each followed by a "double" which is an elaborate variation on the previous dance's chord progression.

Besides being great fun to play, Bach's music is an excellent study in outlining chord progressions with single-note melodies. This piece in particular will help you visualise the CAGED system chord shapes on the neck.

To help you identify common open-position chord shapes, I've included chord symbols where there is a clear progression. Bach uses a range of methods to communicate the harmony, including arpeggios, scales where the chord tones are on strong rhythmic beats, and chromatic approach notes (see the text for Chopin's *Prelude No. 16*).

Bach was an expert at using single notes to articulate a chord progression without sacrificing the lyrical melodic structure. There is a regular contour (the shape of rising and falling melody), but the patterns and intervals are constantly changing, so it never becomes repetitive or predictable. This is the same skill that jazz musicians aim to master, so it's unsurprising that many musicians have respected and studied Bach, including Oscar Peterson, Wynton Marsalis and Esbjörn Svensson.

The Perfect Cadence

Bach lived during the Baroque period of classical music, which is characterised by the importance of harmonic progressions and formal tension and release within a key. Cadences are specific chord changes that create or resolve musical tension.

The most important of these is the *perfect cadence*, which moves from the V chord (a major or dominant 7th chord on the fifth note of the scale) to the tonic or I chord (in both major and minor keys).

For example: G to C, A to Dm, B7 to E, or D7 to Gm.

This progression provides a satisfying resolution of musical tension and often signals the end of a phrase.

Secondary Dominants

The perfect cadence is so strong that additional major or V7 chords can be placed a fifth above other chords to push the music towards a new key. These borrowed chords are known as secondary dominants and Bach loved them! So instead of simply G7 to C major, Bach might add the dominant of G (D) and in turn precede that D with its own dominant (A) and so on. So you could see a sequence like E7 – A – A7 – D – D7 – G – G7 – C!

Visualising Chord Progressions

Visualising shapes on the guitar fretboard is an important skill to develop. It helps us memorise pieces, since understanding the logic of the chord movements helps us to break a piece into phrases and visualise where the notes lie on the fretboard.

Here's a short excerpt of the *Courante* (bars 21-28). Underneath, I've tabbed a chord shape in which the melody can be visualised.

Example 3a:

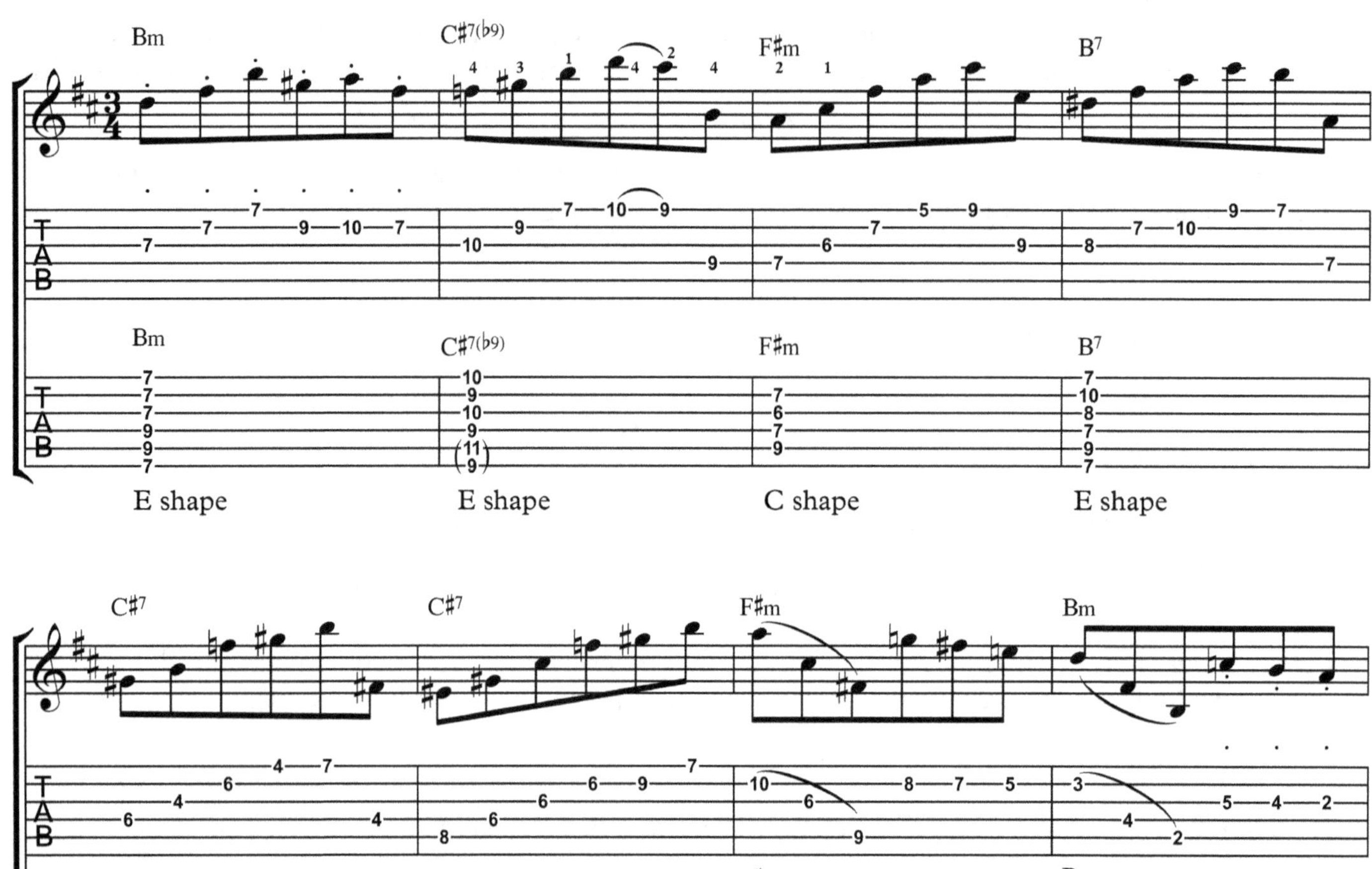

Deciding on the best picking pattern can be tricky. The consideration of string-crossing, tone choice, and tempo are all factors. The *Courante* is not particularly fast but often contains widely spaced string-skipping arpeggios interspersed with scale runs.

Here, I adopt a picking approach where each individual pick stroke is in the direction of the string containing the next note of the arpeggio, and alternate picking for the scale runs. These approaches help accentuate the melody.

Example 3b:

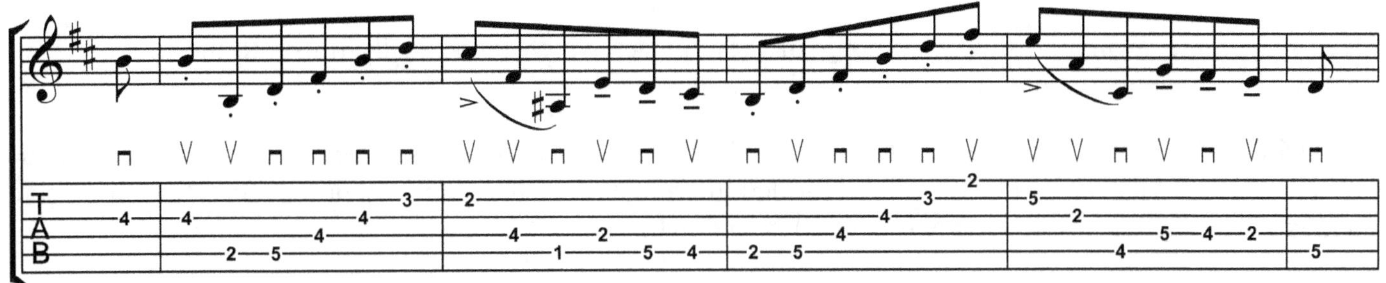

Interview with Dewi Tudor Jones

Dewi has another perspective on interpreting pieces. With Bach in particular, he enthuses about understanding the historic context and phrasing of the dances, as well as harmonic analysis, and how this can help us clearly convey the shape and character to the piece.

DTJ: "I don't think of it as 'interpreting' as much as 'getting to know' it and finding what's in there. Decide how to show that to the listener. Draw their attention to what they need to hear. It's guiding them through it. It's complicated music! So, we need a roadmap through the harmonies."

Dewi doesn't mean literally explain the theory of the harmony to the audience, of course, but by subtle use of rhythm and dynamics you can accentuate the colours, contrasts and developments in the music for non-musicians to pick up on.

DTJ: "If you just play a monotonous string of quavers then the audience will think 'Oh heck, I didn't really make much sense of that.' But if you can point out, 'Here's a colourful chord change, some tension, or a build-up...' There's no actual chords going on but if we can show 'chord change – chord change – chord change – rest' and just lead the listener through it so that they feel what's going on, then I think you've got a successful interpretation.

Follow the contours and look for little sequences. In the first few bars Bach repeats the first phrase a step up, and then up again, then works back down again. If a Romantic composer had written this, they would have written in crescendos and then a diminuendo. [Bach] *didn't write it in, but that's how people would have played it then. They would have seen the step-up through a sequence and then the climb back down."*

I asked Dewi whether our expressive choices boiled down to a combination of rising or falling pitches, and the harmony creating tension or release. When these aspects contradict each other, your own creative judgement has to step in.

DTJ: The common approach is to make stepwise motion legato, and wider leaps staccato. It's a very effective starting point, but not hard and fast. The answers aren't always concrete. Often your guiding principles run against each other. A line might be rising, but also resolving.

The original manuscript contains an unusual pattern of alternating dashed and normal bar lines. This tells us Bach wanted to highlight the two-bar phrasing. Rather than dancing on three beats in each bar, there's a strong beat on the start of bar one, answered by the start of bar two. It doesn't feel like bars of three at all – almost in 2 beats across two bars, with no emphasis on the subdivisions."

Dewi played me two contrasting recordings of these pieces which fantastically illustrate the interpretative ideas you could apply to both of our Bach violin pieces:

Rachael Podger: *Bach: Sonatas & Partitas, Vol. 1* (Channel Classics Records, 2006). Podger plays a Baroque period instrument and has an historically informed interpretation. There are very pronounced staccato/legato contrasts. The rhythm, while secure, is constantly undulating.

Itzhak Perlman: *Bach – Solo Violin Sonatas* (EMI Records, 1988). This features muscular modern playing with less tempo fluctuation and expression. Perlman is much more metronomic and even, but he does still have a sense of phrasing.

Playing Notes:

Bars 1-2 (and throughout): Bach's original manuscript included some phrasing marks, but here I have interpreted them specifically for electric guitar. The phrasing (legato) marks indicate where consecutive notes should ring as a chord. Lightly palm mute the staccato notes. This gives several distinct colours to the solo guitar texture, especially with a slightly overdriven tone.

Bar 8: This chromatic phrase is a real finger-twister. My suggested fingerings may take time to feel natural, but they help the line to flow without your hand leaping all over the fretboard.

Bar 10: This Bsus4 chord is tricky to play cleanly without disturbing the melodic flow. At first, separate the chord into two parts: the B power chord can be played with a downstroke, then hybrid pick the high E with your second finger. Rake from low to high rather than attempting to play all three notes simultaneously.

Bars 22-26: This section's interesting phrasing can be brought out with some rubato. Many violin performances lean on the last note of bar 22 and the first of bar 23, giving a heavy "& 1" pick-up into each bar before speeding up again. This gives contrast to the bass notes and the impression of two players answering each other.

Bars 27-28: The G in bar 27 and C natural in bar 28 is the flat 2nd which prevents the melody fully resolving into the keys of F# Minor or B Minor. The G in bar 27 nudges F# minor into the role of a minor V chord which resolves to B minor. The C in bar 28 then undermines B minor as the tonic chord, instead implying that it is chord iii in the key of G Major.

In rock, Joe Satriani is credited with the concept of "pitch axis", where a single chord or note is used in two or more roles and the music rotates around it (as in his songs *Satch Boogie* and *Flying in a Blue Dream*).

Bars 32-33: The piece started in the key of B Minor, and bars 32-33 now set up the return to the introduction with a perfect cadence (V-i) from F#7. In this context, C#7 is a secondary dominant, meaning that it performs the same perfect cadence onto the V chord. Secondary dominants can be chained together to heighten the eventual resolution, as in the common jazz chord progression III-VI-II-V-I.

In harmony numerals, C#7 can be written as either II7 or V7/V, since C# is technically the 2nd note in the key of B Minor, but is temporarily behaving as the 5th of F#.

Bars 34-42: The B section starts on F# major. The fingerings will need individual practice but the general principle of held chords and short scale runs is business as usual by this point.

Bars 44-46: Another tricky targeting phrase. The open strings make it much more palatable, but leave the picking hand to cope with some wide string skipping.

Bars 49-50: Bach is treading water reinforcing E minor before resolving, but notice the well-placed D# on beat 3 of both bars. This provides just enough of a kick to stop the E minor getting too static and losing momentum.

Bar 54: These 10th intervals (see notes on Paganini's *16th Caprice*) can be interpreted in multiple ways. The first 10th interval might function as the 3rd and 5th of D major, the second as the b7 and 5th of A7, and the third as root and 3rd of D major. Another interpretation is that there are two voices playing call-and-response as they both descend through the scale. The genius of Bach is that densely packed chord progressions are smuggled under the radar by such smooth melodic passages.

Bars 61-62: This IV-V-I cadence in D Major (G, A, D chords) resolves particularly well. In the audio demo, notice how I put emphasis on the D in bar 62 before moving into the next phrase. Use your ear to help decide where similar "resting points" lie throughout the piece.

Bars 74-77: There are some nice comfortable scales here, again targeting the root note E in bar 75. The following two bars simply repeat up two frets. Alternate pick the scale runs but hybrid pick the arpeggios in bars 75 and 77. I try to milk the drama of these phrases by rushing down the scales then dragging the tempo on the open voice triads, especially on the repeat.

Bar 79 to End: There are more straightforward phrases to end. Bars 79 and 80 target the notes of F#7, but in a more linear way than before. The B minor arpeggio to finish has some grace notes that aren't in the original score, but helped me capture the same aesthetic that violin players would get. There is a big Yngwie-style vibrato at the end.

You could take some liberties the second time around, just to let everyone know you've got to the end. Improvising a flashy cadenza was quite the done thing in the Baroque period, so you could extend the B minor arpeggio with some of your favourite sweep-picking licks!

Partita No. 1 in B minor: III. Courante – J.S. Bach

23
F♯m
B7
C♯7
C♯7
F♯m
TAB
28
Bm
G
E♯o7
C♯7
F♯7
dim.
33
F♯7
Bm
B7
let ring
mp
39
Em
E7
Am
Ao7
B7
Em

44
B7
Em
E7
Am
B7
49
Em
E
A
Bm
E7
54
A7
D
A7
D
A7
59
D7
G
A
D
A
D
F♯7

64
Bm
C♯7
F♯7
G♯m
F♯m

69
Em
E7
C♯o7
Bm
F♯
P.M.

74
E7
A
F♯7
B7(♭9)
P.M.
P.M.

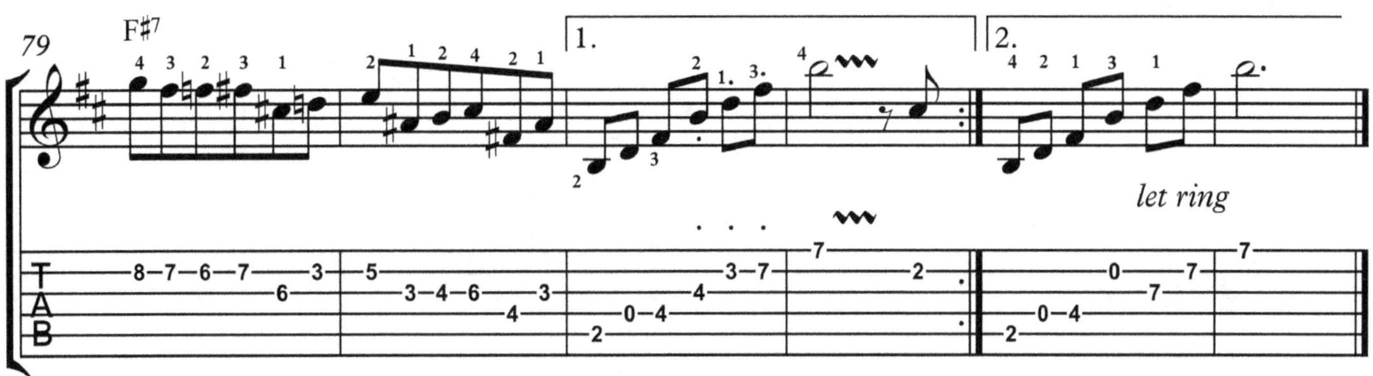
79
F♯7
1.
2.
let ring

Chapter Four – *Violin Partita No. 1 in B Minor (VI. Double)* (J.S. Bach)

Here's the sixth movement from Bach's *Partita No. 1 in B Minor* for solo violin. As mentioned earlier, this suite has a typical baroque structure of four dances, each followed by a development called a "double" which takes the structure and harmony of the dance but adds more embellishment and instrumental virtuosity.

This "double" occurs after the *Sarabande* (movement V), which is a Spanish dance with Arabic traits. The dance was considered quite provocative in the early Baroque period but this may well have been historic by Bach's time.

Listen to recordings of the *Sarabande* and this double to see how they compare. The main differences are the faster tempo and change of time signature. The *Sarabande* is in 3/4, mostly using crotchets with occasional quavers, while the double is in 9/8 and maintains a relentless triplet-style phrasing. Hearing the less-elaborate movement V will also help you to decide on appropriate rhythmic phrasing.

Closed voicings vs. Open Voicings

The violin, being tuned in 5ths and having a short scale length, facilitates much wider chord shapes compared with the guitar's 4ths tuning and longer scale. When describing chord voicings, the phrases "closed-voice" and "open-voice" refer to the spread of notes. This is separate from an "inversion" which refers only to the order of notes, and chiefly which note is at the top or bottom of the chord.

The notation below makes the difference clearer. Closed voicings have all the necessary notes in order with no gaps, while an open voicing displaces at least one note by an octave creating gaps in the sequence.

You might recognise these shapes as being part of already familiar chord shapes. By omitting certain notes from those big barre chords, the sound becomes open and more easily blended with other instruments, or more exciting when used melodically, because of the wider interval leaps.

Both bars in the example below contain three inversions of C major. Those in the first bar are spaced as close as possible, whereas in the second bar the notes are spread further apart. Notice how the chords in both bars have the same bass notes.

Example 4a:

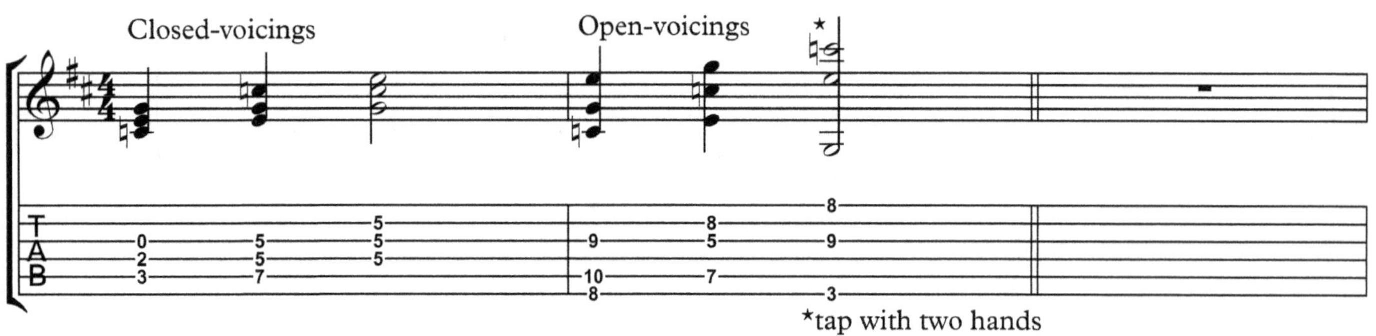

Open-voiced triads have an airy sound that provides harmony without sounding dense and muddy. You can hear open-voiced triads used melodically in Eric Johnson's *Cliffs of Dover* (opening solo) and as accompaniment in Sting's *Shape of My Heart,* played by Dominic Miller.

Barre-rolls vs. Stacked Fingers

There are many instances in this piece where notes at the same fret are required on two adjacent strings. This poses a problem and guitarists tend to favour one of two fingering options. The first is using one finger for both, rolling from the fingertip on one string to the pad on the next string. This is known as a "barre-roll". The second option is to stack multiple fingers, each playing one string.

The following exercises explore both approaches. Each bar is repeated first with fingerings for barre-rolls and then stacked fingers. The barre-roll is achieved by arm/elbow movement. It works best on two strings and is particularly tricky for three or more strings, or if skipping a string is required. To avoid bleeding between the notes, palm mute the lower string as you pick the higher one. Barre-rolls work best with a square-on fretting hand position, while stacking will benefit from a bluesier angled hand position.

Example 4b:

Each has its pros and cons. Barre-rolling is tricky and risks notes bleeding into one another, while stacking fingers cramps the hand position and ties up several fingers, making it difficult to transition to the next phrase. Ultimately, it is good to have some facility with both options while acknowledging your strengths. With this in mind, explore my recommended fingerings but feel free to change them.

Check out the supporting video content to see my exact fretting hand positions.

Leapfrog Picking

This piece occasionally requires some tricky double string skips. The following exercise will help you target these areas and do wonders for your overall picking dexterity. Play with downstrokes, instead of "true" sweep picking i.e., each note is an individual stroke while the forearm moves the picking hand across the strings).

You can check out the videos to see these exercises performed.

Example 4c:

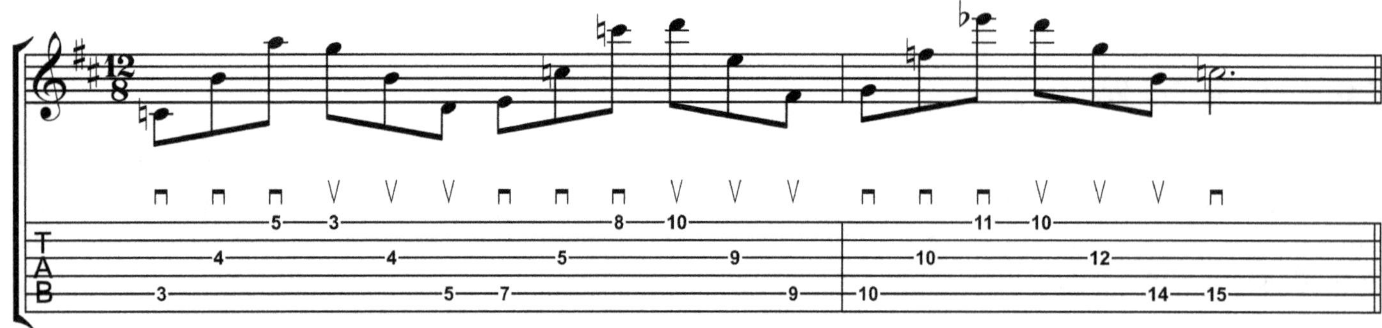

Interview with Dewi Tudor Jones (pt.2)

Compared with Romantic composers like Chopin, Bach added very few performance directions to his scores. Partly because the elements of music notation were developing, but also because he understood that musicians of the Baroque period were much more familiar with the forms, intended variation and improvisation.

DTJ: "It's funny isn't it? When you're starting out it looks like a dreadful piece of music. It just looks like a page of quavers. But you just have to start making sense of it. The first thing is to work out where the phrases [begin and end]. *They're not always in obvious places.*

You need to remember these are all dances and, particularly when you play the doubles, you should listen to what it's the double of. It helps you work out what is important, what you want to hear. This double is just a decoration of the Saraband [plays the tune from movement V. *Saraband*]. *Try to carry the sense of rhythm over from the dance to the double."*

Since the piece is a continuous line of 1/8th note triplets, it can be easy to neglect the 9/8 time signature. However, the cycle of three beats-per-bar aligns with the chord changes and, if observed, will give the piece its characteristic rhythmic bounce. Test yourself by counting aloud "1, 2, 3" as you play and accent the first beat of each bar with a heavier pick stroke, or take Dewi's advice and get your full body moving with the main beats in each bar.

"Whenever I'm playing music like this, I always try to have this 'rolling through the bars' feeling. In Baroque music the first beat is always strongest, the second is lighter and the third propels us into the next bar. Remember it's a dance – think of the steps. It's concert music rather than music for actually dancing to, but it's taken from a dance genre. So, when you're playing [the piece], *it's nice to imagine how someone might dance to it."*

Comparing this double to movement V, the *Saraband* will also clarify what the underlying chord progression is.

DTJ: "As well as noticing what's important in the melody, the other thing you're doing here is that you're playing all the counterpoint yourself. The counterpoint is hidden away within this one melodic line. You're doing melody and bassline at once."

Playing Notes:

Bar 5: The first of many intricate picking sections. Follow the suggested fingerings to avoid the fretting hand getting in a tangle. The stacked fingers on beat 1 help to keep the hand in position for the rest of the bar. Memorise in short chunks until the fingering is smooth and natural.

Bar 8: As with the previous piece, Bach gets busy decorating the chord progressions. Here an F#7 chord leads us back to the B Minor of bar one. Try to identify fragments of chord shapes.

Bar 10: The A section began on B minor (the tonic) and ended on F#7 (the dominant). By contrast, the B section starts on F#7 and works towards B minor, just like in the *Courante*. The two sections both journey away from, then return to, the tonic chord.

Bar 14: This might just be the toughest bar of the piece! The repeated use of third and fourth fingers means unwanted ringing open strings are likely. Once the fingering and picking are coming together, keep things quiet both by laying the first finger flat and also using palm muting.

Beat 2 of bar 14 has an awkward position shift to the 4th fret. Rotating the wrist away from you as the hand moves down the neck will bring the second finger up to the D string, then rotate back in again as the second finger moves to the B string. There isn't one correct fretting-hand position, my hand often changes angle several times during a single phrase.

Bars 17-19: Spot the ii-V-I. These three bars move through E minor, A7 and D major. The 9/8 time-signature means that the accentuated notes fall in groups of three. The A7 and D major chords have chord tones on each beat with two passing notes in between.

Bar 20: This ascending G major arpeggio is another high-risk manoeuvre. The two notes on the G string hinder sweep/leapfrog picking, so use alternate picking. The first finger propels the hand up the neck during the three position-shifts.

Bars 26-29: Bach recycles a two-bar phrase by transposing it up a tone. The pattern in bar 26 is slightly altered to fit the key in bar 28.

Bar 30: Use two downstrokes and the second finger to pluck the E string, to stop you tripping over the repeated string skips. Accent the lowest of each group of three notes to propel the music forward and highlight the three quick chord changes in this bar.

Bars 32-33: Target the notes of B minor from a semitone below before playing the longer arpeggio. Notice how similar this ending is to the *Courante*. Similar motifs are used in the other movements, and the whole *Partita* is really taking one main idea and reinterpreting it in each of the baroque dances.

Bar 34 to End: I've sneaked in a few extra grace notes and ended with a natural harmonic at the 19th fret that's played with the picking hand. If you're lucky enough to get the harmonic and the fretted B string ringing together, use your picking hand to smoothly dampen first the B string, then the E string. The effect should be as if fading into a mellow, octave-up feedback.

Partita No. 1 in B minor: VI. Double – J.S. Bach

19
22
25
28
31
1.
2.
let ring
N.H.

Chapter Five – *Park* (Nate Chivers)

Nate Chivers is a composer, arranger and guitarist from Western Massachusetts, now based in Central Florida, USA. As a composer, his music is often described as contemplative and playful. It is also a reflection of his rock, pop, jazz and classical influences, amongst many others.

As a composer he has worked with Psappha, sitarist Jasdeep Singh-Degun, tubist Jack Adler-McKean, members of the Royal Scottish National Symphony, BBC Singers, Music Theatre Wales and CoMA. He is currently an Associate Composer with the UnHeard Music Collective and arranger for the Sonos Ensemble.

He was also the arranger and guitarist for the Manchester Video Game Orchestra from 2019-2022. His music been performed in the USA, UK, France and China, as well as being featured on BBC Radio 3.

His album *Nowhere to Hide* is an exploration of intimacy and fragility through the lens of solo electric guitar. By using unorthodox techniques, it makes a unique contribution to guitar literature while remaining musically accessible.

Chivers composed the set of solo pieces from which *Park* is taken with a firm ethos of no effects, no loops, no overdubs – just clean electric guitar played with a pick; a total simplicity of resources. From these limitations he has expanded the sound palette by avoiding the usual rock guitar techniques.

When I asked Chivers what made these pieces explicitly "electric", given the lack of any sound-processing, swells, bends or whammy bar antics, he enthused about the subtleties of sound that one can coax only from an electric guitar, thanks to the inherent compression and resonance in the pickups. *Park*, in particular, is born from the subtle pitches present in muted notes, contrasted with ringing harmonics. Both would be impossible on an acoustic guitar without unnaturally close mic-ing or a magnetic pickup.

N.C: "The string skipping in general is hard enough, but then not to actually press with your fingers takes quite some getting used to. Guitarists tend to follow our fretting fingers, meaning that the picking dexterity is being synced to the fretting-hand placement (notice how string skipping feels trickier on open strings). When you're not pressing down, it's a less decisive movement for your picking hand to sync to. It feels like you're a ballerina or a gymnast, just balancing on the tips. Some guitar playing is like sprinting or brute force, but here you have to be so exact, light, and agile."

For Chivers, a big challenge to performing *Park* was just memorising it:

NC: "The piece is like a set of variations on the same motif that changes every time. And you do have to memorise it, because it's too fast to read and the light touch is too precarious. You can't do it by feel while looking at sheet music because you're never actually touching down onto frets to get a good reference point.

It's all pretty much in the same area but it's so quick and involves a lot of darting back and forth between the lowest and highest strings. The amount of changes of hand position call for a similar mindset to playing advanced jazz chords, but then it's this simple I-IV-V piece."

Chivers performs *Park* exclusively with a pick, so the lesson notes are written with that in mind. However, feel free to explore a hybrid-picking or even fingerstyle approach.

Park is on the 2022 album *Nowhere to Hide,* available on Bandcamp. Nate's upcoming album blends the experimental new sounds from the first album with more conventional electric guitar playing.

Listen at **www.natechivers.bandcamp.com/** About: **www.nchiverscomposer.com**

Harmonics

Several of Chivers' pieces feature advanced natural and artificial harmonics. First inspired as a teenager by guitarist Matthias Eklundh, Chivers has developed a vocabulary of double-stop harmonics at hard-to-reach frets, as well as the common harmonics at the 12th, 7th and 5th frets.

Due to the discrepancies in equal temperament tuning, you'll find that harmonics below the 5th fret are not exactly aligned to the frets. The 4th fret harmonics are slightly behind the fret, while the 3rd fret ones are in front (around fret 3.2).

Muted Notes

The melody notes are performed muted and are played by laying the finger on the string without pressing the fret. However, there is still pitch content present in these dead notes and Chivers exploits this to bring a new texture to the tune.

When you're softly deadening the string and not fully fretting the notes, intonation becomes an issue, just like playing the violin. When jumping back and forth to the low harmonics, it may take time for the fingers to land exactly over the fret wire and will require considerable practice.

Use two fingers on the string where possible when you're muting, as placing one finger behind your "fretting" finger (especially behind notes at the 7th or 5th frets) will avoid accidental harmonics.

Normally, a muted note is written with an X in the TAB but in *Park* the pitches are crucial, so fret numbers are needed. Aside from the free-time bridge and coda, all the notes on the three thinnest strings will be muted. If you're unsure whether a particular note should be a harmonic or muted, just glance up at the stave and check for a diamond (harmonic) or a cross (mute) note head.

Fretting-hand Position

If you struggle to swap between the harmonics and muted notes, it may be because you're trying to fret both with the same hand shape. Break *Park* up into its components and notice how your hand naturally wants to play them. As you combine the components of the piece, remain aware of the change as you practice.

Playing Notes:

Bars 1-2: You encounter every main challenge of this piece straight away. Keep the thumb low on the back of the neck to arch the fretting fingers, so that the harmonics don't mute each other. As the muted melody note is on the 5th fret you should use two fingers.

Bar 6: To keep the score clear and neat, I've avoided writing excessive tied notes to keep the score tidy, but in general the harmonics should be allowed to ring i.e., bar five's harmonics should still be heard in bar six.

Bars 7-10: Break the tune down into short sections. It will help if you play the melody as regular fretted notes at first and focus only on the harmonics. The better you know the tune, the better your intonation will be when you add the muting.

Bars 15-17: While Nate's suggestion of keeping two fingers on the string when muting to avoid unwanted harmonics is good advice, there are certain phrases where this is more easily said than done and it's easier to dampen the note by palm muting. Fretting the 5th and 9th frets is a comfortable stretch with your first and fourth finger, but risks an unwanted harmonic at the 5th fret. However, if the second finger is used at the 5th fret, then you'll need to adjust your forearm, elbow and shoulder to make the extra position shifts.

Bar 22: The mutes at the 6th fret aren't likely to make harmonics, but let the first finger extend onto the G string behind the second finger to subdue a potential harmonic at the 7th fret.

Bars 23-25: The harmonics can be allowed to ring out as much as possible to contrast with the staccato muted melody, especially in these bars when they form chords. Bounce the fingers quickly off the harmonics to avoid dampening adjacent strings.

The audio includes Chivers' original album recording. Listen closely and hear how to pace these slow 1/2 note triplets correctly. They're slower than you think.

Bars 34-35: There are some tricky chords here. Use your first finger for muting by barring behind the notes (like bars 15-17) and use the remaining fingers for the chords. The first finger can then leap across to the low E string for the harmonic.

Bars 36-38: These are the trickiest harmonics in this piece. Remember that "3rd fret" really means slightly in front of the fret. Find where this harmonic is on your instrument and practice 5th, 4th and 3rd-fret harmonics on each string. They should make a pleasing major arpeggio. Plucking closer to the bridge helps any shy natural harmonics to pop out.

Bars 43-46: The muted notes should be played with your middle and fourth fingers, once again shadowed by the first finger. The 7th fret harmonics then use the third finger. Once memorised, focus on your hand position to make it fluid. A smooth wrist rotation should help extend the third finger's reach, allowing you to move smoothly back and forth between the two shapes. Enjoy the simplicity of bar 46, but don't be tempted to dig in harder. These chords should sound just like the others even though there's no melody.

Bars 47-50: These four bars are a breath of fresh air and bring some much needed calm after the driving tempo. Chivers encourages some creative interpretation here: you can play the harmonics fast or slow, with pauses between them or without. Just be sure that they contrast with the rest of the piece.

Bar 65: The final bar returns to the free-time harmonic arpeggios. As the technique gets easier, you should consider some expressive interpretation. Record the ending at different speeds and with different rhythms to decide exactly how you'd like to shape it. A sudden stark contrast to the previous bars, or a gradual slowing from the main tempo, would both work – it's up to you.

Park – Nate Chivers

19
23
27
31

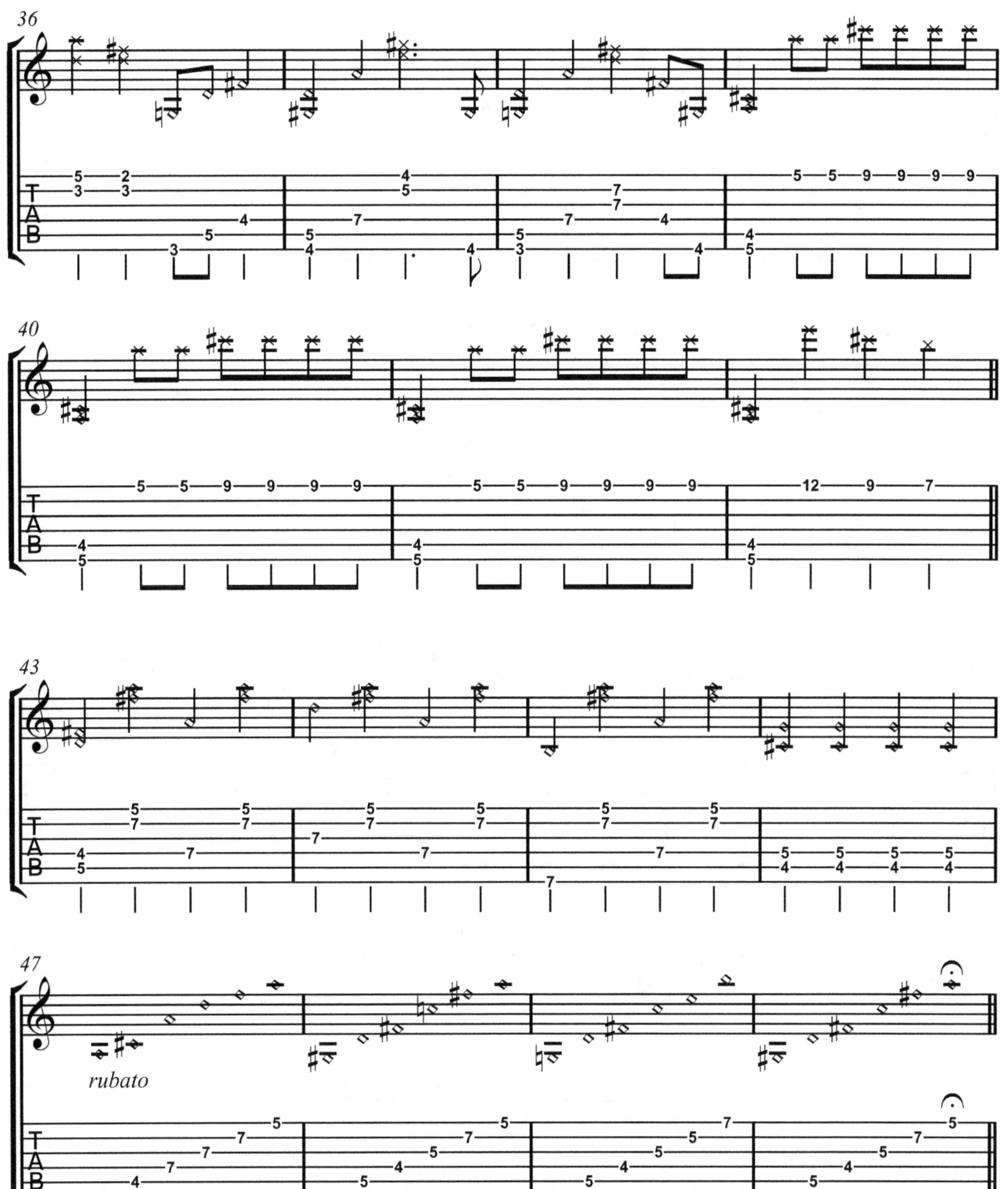
36
40
43
47
rubato

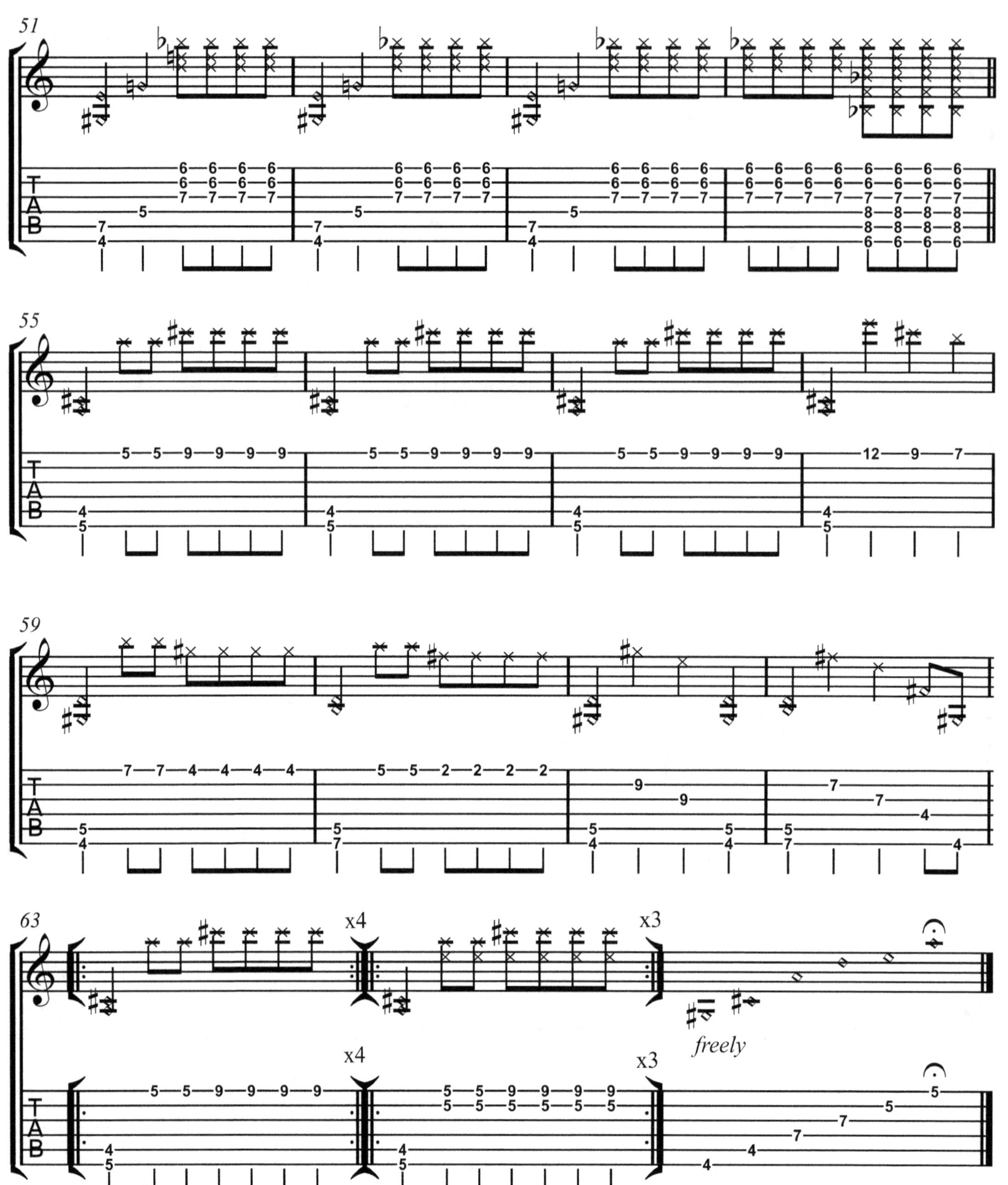
51
55
59
63
x4
x3
freely

Chapter Six – *Caprice No. 16 in G Minor* (Niccolò Paganini)

Niccolò Paganini (1782-1840) was one of the main inspirations of the '80s neoclassical shred movement. Born in Genoa, Paganini was recognised as a child prodigy, and was touring Europe by the age of 18. His lasting legacy is as a virtuosic instrumentalist and flamboyant performer, but Paganini also studied composition and published many violin-focused works.

Among his best-known compositions are a set of twenty-four caprices for unaccompanied violin. The 5th and 24th caprices in particular have become test pieces for shred guitarists and you can find renditions by Jason Becker, Chris Impellitteri, Andy James and Steve Vai. In fact, the legends of Paganini's turbulent rock-star behaviour and exhaustive 15-hour practice routines make him practically the archetype for late '80s virtuoso shred guitarists.

Yngwie Malmsteen has acknowledged the influence of Paganini on his music and has performed an excerpt from Paganini's *4th Violin Concerto* in concert. Here we'll be looking at the *16th Caprice in G Minor*.

Playing Paganini's pieces on guitar challenges our technique and fretboard knowledge. Violins are tuned in fifths which, together with the much shorter scale length, allows wider intervals to fall easily under the fingers. To keep up with "the devil's violinist" the transcription uses a mixture of advanced rock guitar techniques that include sweep picking, hybrid picking, legato and tapping.

Paganini's masterful use of arpeggios and chord tone targeting allows the solo melody to imply a clear chord progression. Visualising the chord shapes that each phrase draws upon will help you to memorise the piece and also to carry over ideas into your own vocabulary. Analyse the note choice (arpeggios, scales, wide intervals, chromatic notes, etc) as you work through the arrangement and look for patterns or sequences.

Hybrid Picking

Skipping several strings with alternate picking requires a lot of accuracy so hybrid picking (using pick and finger) gives much better economy of motion and helps with accuracy at high speeds.

The first bar of Example 7a introduces the hybrid picking approach that's used throughout the piece. The second bar combines this with sweep picking to help you tackle bar thirteen. Keep the picking hand in the same position for the sweep that you then use for plucking with the second finger.

Example 6a:

Tenth Intervals

The Bach *Partita* earlier in the book featured occasional 10th (a 3rd plus an octave) intervals but this caprice features entire phrases built on them so they're worth some attention. As with 3rds, 10ths can be major or minor.

Example 6b:

Playing Notes:

Bars 1-8: The opening section introduces many of the ideas that recur throughout the piece, so it's worth spending time memorising and practicing these before tackling the rest of the tune.

Bar one outlines a G minor triad with a short embellishment around the root before descending. Bar two moves to D7. After a short pedal-point lick, the melody leaps up to begin a descending arpeggio from the root (D) before switching to a diminished seventh arpeggio in bar three.

Bar 2: As indicated in the picking directions, tackle these phrases with hybrid picking.

Bar 5: The previous pedal-point motif is recycled in bar five, this time over G7, signalling a key change to C Minor. However, this is immediately undermined by the following arpeggios which outline F and Bb chords and reveal a ii-V-I sequence in Bb Major.

Bar 6: These wide intervals are particularly unfriendly on guitar. Take time to master the combination of **m** and **m & a** plucking. The position of the picking hand is crucial, so build up the movement slowly.

Bars 12-13: Juggling these two-note fragments in different registers of the instrument is one of the most difficult sections of the piece. Memorise the shifts slowly to ensure you have the most economic approach and follow the picking directions closely.

Bars 15-20: This scale-based passage includes a lot of chromatic notes but should feel easier than the previous few bars' gymnastics. Using legato here can provide a nice break from pick attack, both for you and for the listener!

Bar 18: Several fingerings are viable for this big position shift. I used a rather extreme barre-roll to jump across five strings. Flatten the first finger when playing the low A string then angle it back to fret the high E with the base of the finger, at the same time as sliding from the 8th fret to the 12th.

Bars 21-26: Back to sweep/hybrid-picking. Paganini has combined an arpeggio with some chromatic passing notes and answered it with a pedal-point lick over the next chord. He moves from Bb to F7 to A diminished then back to Bb in the second two bars. The A diminished triad functions here as an F7b9 which resolves to Bb.

Bars 35-38: The tonal contrast between the descending 10th intervals and the denser ascending arpeggio patterns can be heightened with some change of tempo and dynamics. Start lightly then gradually dig in to crescendo on the descent before ascending quickly and loudly.

Bars 46-49: A flurry of descending chromatic notes finishes the piece. It is played as legato as possible from the start of the section to help transition into the two-handed tapping. The wide jumps to the high D and F# in bars 48-49 are handled by tapping with the second and third fingers of the picking hand. Flatten any spare fretting hand fingers against the strings to mute unwanted noise while keeping the third finger free to hammer on to the E string.

Bars 50-51: The previous motif is transposed to G minor. Keep using second or third fingers to tap throughout while adjusting the angle of the hand to suit each two-note shape.

Bar 52 to End: If you're playing this track with any distortion the final chord will be a muddy mess, so during the legato phrase use your picking hand or a pedal to roll off the volume. This will bring out a warm G minor chord that leaves the listener with a sweeter impression.

Niccolò Paganini – Caprice No. 16 in G Minor

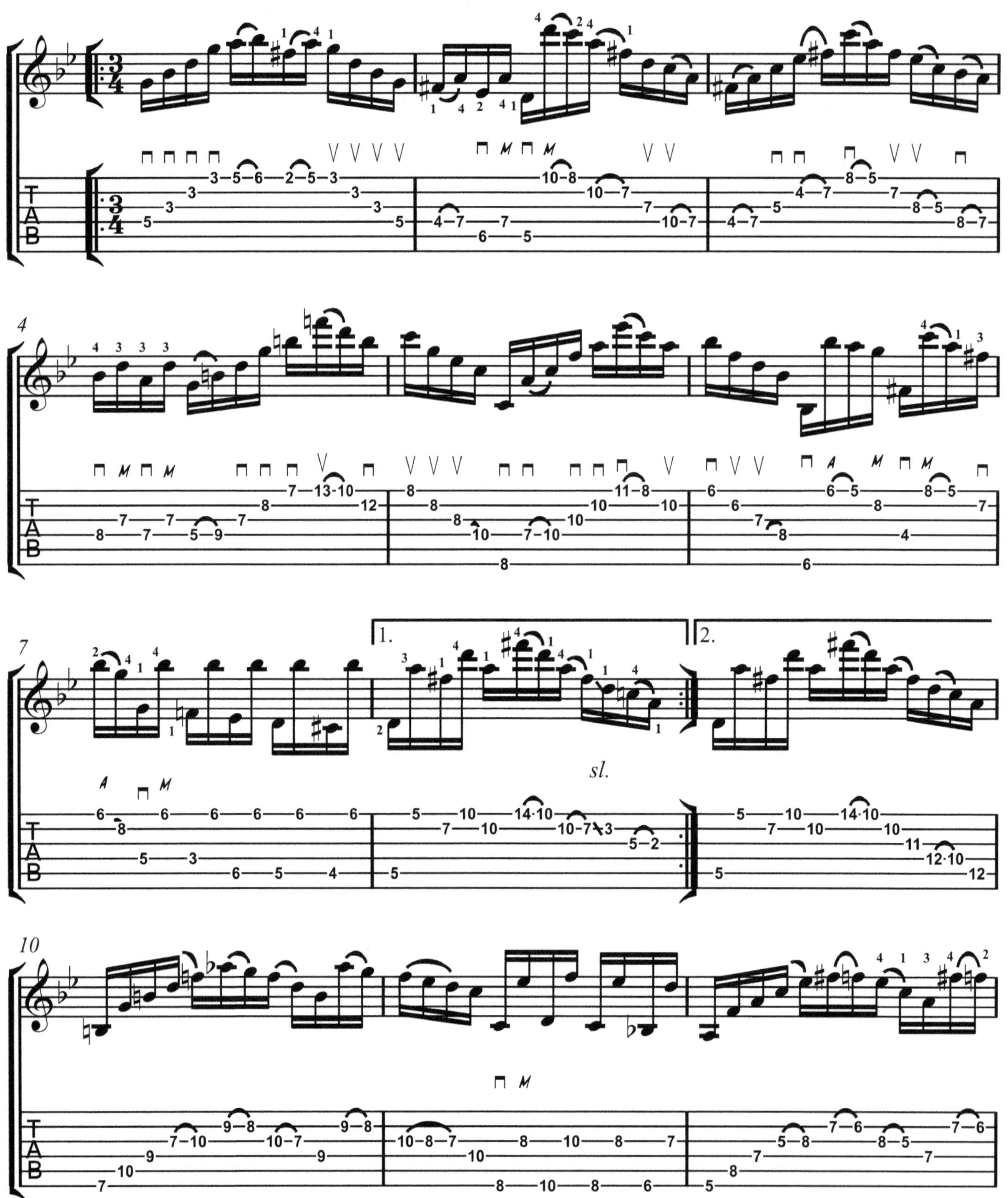

26

29

32

38

41

44
47

51
T
A
B

Chapter Seven – Liverpool Counterpoint (Rob Thorpe)

I composed this piece for this book and took inspiration from several artists who work in the borderlands between contemporary classical music and rock. It uses a loop pedal to create a thicker polyphonic texture and create a "backing track", but I'd argue that the loops are created during the performance, so no outside accompaniment is required.

One of the most influential strands of classical music in the 20th century has been the Minimalism movement. These composers were reacting to the a-rhythmic dissonance that dominated new academic music between the 1930s and 1970s, and instead used gradually changing layers of repetitive patterns, consonant tonality, regular tempos, tape loops and electronic effects. All of which sound familiar to the present day rock guitarist.

Steve Reich is one of minimalism's best-known composers, (although he prefers to call it "gradual process music"). Reich was associated with the San Francisco Tape Music Centre, an experimental music facility in the 1960s that connected composers to the experimental art- and rock-music scenes. Reich's first experiments were to loop two identical tapes but at fractionally different speeds. These phasing experiments were then reimagined for groups of live musicians, eventually leading to his 1987 composition *Electric Counterpoint*, first performed by jazz guitarist Pat Metheny.

Tape is the ancestor of modern digital looper pedals and one of the first rock musicians to harness this technology to perform looped music in real time was King Crimson's Robert Fripp. He designed a setup of tape recorders, dubbed *Frippertronics,* and demonstrated the influence of the *avant-garde* feeding back into rock music.

While pop music initially influenced minimalism, the inspirational flow became two-way. By the '80s, space rock had embraced electronic effects and swirling textures, before progressive rock and metal embraced intricate cross rhythmic patterns and odd meters. Finally, '90s post-rock plunged into a sea of gradually changing riffs, long-form structures, and great waves of sound.

This grey area where progressive rock, experimental music, contemporary classical, post-rock and noise converged has pushed the electric guitar to some of its most unconventional and extreme roles.

In particular, Glenn Branca wrote "symphonies" for orchestras of electric guitarists and, in the last 15 years, British band Ex-Easter Island Head have explored unique guitar *preparations* to create their own hybrid rock/minimalist classical music.

A quick online search will return a huge amount of music made with loop pedals. I especially recommend Argentinian/Icelandic duo Hungría (*Cumbre de Nieves Perpetuas*, 2019), bassist Steve Lawson (*Grace and Gratitude*, 2004) and solo cellist Polly Virr (*Solace* EP, 2023)

The piece *Liverpool Counterpoint* is my homage to all these artists, and draws together texture, layered rhythms, guitar preparations and manipulating effects in three contrasting movements.

Loop music can sometimes become boring and predictable once the novelty of its construction has worn off. The key to maintaining interest is generating many different textures, using either physical techniques or effects. *Liverpool Counterpoint* includes volume swells, bowing the strings with an Allen key (hex wrench) and tapped/natural harmonics to keep the timbre varied.

If you are new to looping, then I highly recommend the Fundamental Changes book *Guitar Looping: The Creative Guide* by Kristof Neyens.

When looping, the crucial skill is to synchronise the tapping of your foot to the downbeat of your playing. At first, it is surprisingly tricky to activate the pedal and strum exactly at the same moment. The more consistent your internal sense of tempo, the easier it will be to overdub each additional layer.

The first loop you record is the crucial "timing loop". This primary loop dictates the time period within which the subsequent overdubs repeat. If you are starting with a repeating pattern, it is helpful to play it a few times before hitting record to settle your tempo and create a confident groove.

This two-layer example is a good test of your rhythm skills and synchronisation. Use big strumming motions to help steady your timing. Repeat the first bar several times before tapping the pedal to begin recording. Then see if you can do a "cold start", recording straight away on the first note.

Example 7a:

Looping Notation

There is currently no consensus regarding written notation for effect pedals, or to describe how they should be controlled during a performance, so composers often refer to pictures or lengthy written descriptions. To streamline the score for *Liverpool Counterpoint*, I use symbols taken from audio/visual equipment, as follows:

RECORD

Start the loop pedal (initiating the primary timing loop).

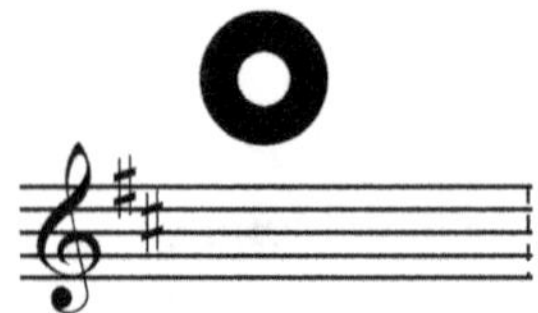

PLAYBACK

Close a loop/stop recording and start playback (note: some pedals directly switch from record to overdub mode).

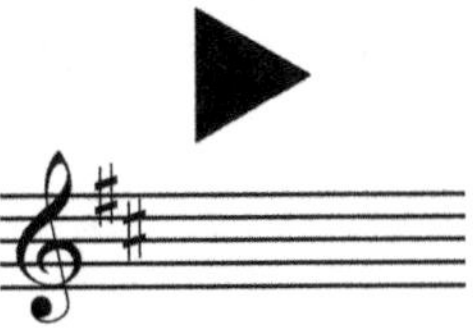

OVERDUB

Start recording an overdub (this symbol is similar to RECORD but since a new loop can't be started without first stopping all loop playback, the context where the symbol is used will avoid any misunderstanding).

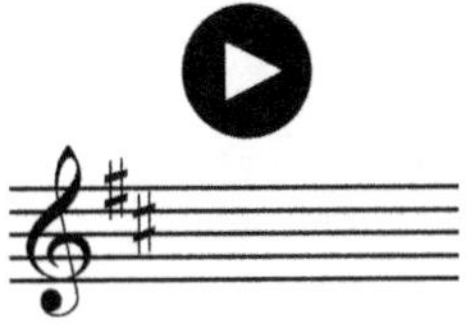

STOP PLAYBACK

Stop all loop playback, deleting previous recordings (on compact pedals, this usually involves a double-tap or tap-and-hold).

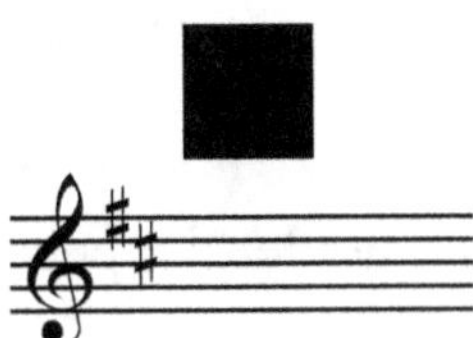

The Allen-key Bow

One of my favourite sounds on the electric guitar is created by bowing the strings with an Allen key (hex wrench). Holding the tool between thumb and two fingers (I use middle and ring) parallel to the frets, saw gently across the strings to produce an ethereal, synth-pad-like sound.

The fret over which you bow dictates the pitch. Rubbing in a circular motion around the fret provides vibrato. Bow all the strings at first, but you'll find that you can angle the Allen key to just bow a selection of strings as your control improves.

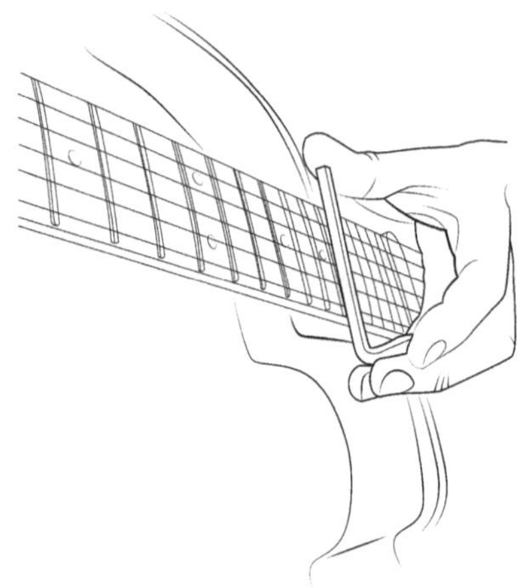

Playing Notes:

Tuning: Drop-D tuning

Movement I:

Bars 1-4: Bar lengths and numbers are approximate throughout the first movement and are included for ease of reference, as an even pulse is all that matters. The exact number of notes should vary in order to ensure the staggered entry and exit of each overdub. This initial loop should last roughly 20-25 seconds, including some space at the start and end to allow for the overdubs.

Bar 5: Depending on your loop pedal, it might immediately start overdubbing when you close the initial loop. If so, there's no need to rush straight into the next phrase. Once you start to hear the first line coming in, leave a few beats then start to play the D notes. I faded each line in using a volume pedal (placed before the looper) but you could just use a gradual pick attack.

Bar 8: Once you're overdubbing there's no need to start/stop recording between phrases. Just let the pedal keep recording but be careful of making any unwanted noise.

Bars 11-16: Keep adding layers until you have a rich collage of different pulsating tones. This first section might seem simplistic, but it takes experience to stagger the different layers so that they fade in and out in regular rotation.

Bar 17: Set the pedal to "Playback" then chill out, letting everyone bask in your handiwork before moving on to the next section.

Bars 18-21: Start strumming very quietly so that the C# minor can barely be heard through the mix, then crescendo gradually. Stop the loop playback when you're playing the loudest you can, but continue playing the new chord. Then strum more quietly and reduce the range of the strumming until you're just picking the D string.

During this transition you will need to delete the stored audio, so the pedal is ready to start recording a fresh loop. When you're relaxed and confident, start recording the next new loop. Note, this section doesn't leave any rests in the first loop of notes – it is a constant pulse of about 15 seconds of C#s.

Bars 22-30: Repeat the same process as bar 1-17 with the new sequence of notes, leaving gaps between entries in the overdubs, as in bars 5-16.

Bars 31-33: Make sure you've got the Allen key to hand in advance. See the main text and supporting video for more description. Once you've stopped the loop, start to lean the Allen key over, so it just bows the higher strings, and eventually just the E string before coming to the end.

Movement II:

Bars 34-37: Set the tempo confidently during the first two bars then record the second two bars to get the best chance of a solid take. This section involves more precise interlocking rhythms, so nailing this initial timing loop is essential. Even when performing, keep repeating the riff until you feel confident recording.

Bars 38-45: The repeat bars indicate that you should overdub each new layer then tap Playback to generate the repeat. Alternatively, you could play the first repeat without recording, then record the second take.

Bar 39: This section of the piece gradually constructs a two-bar phrase of continuous 1/8th notes, but because we're playing them one at a time, they can be sustained. You can play about with how many notes you choose to sustain and for how long. Be aware that too many ringing notes might start to mask the melody.

Bar 47: After one repeat, let the loop play back about three more times. It's not essential to hit the Playback in time – it's better to leave it late, so as not to cut short the F# in bar 47.

Bar 48: This moment requires some adept multitasking. Stop the previous loop (and delete it) while simultaneously launching into a new riff at the much faster tempo of about 170 bpm. First, learn the riff in isolation. Then learn to estimate and commit to the tempo change. It will help to play along to my demo recording (without your looper).

Bars 52-63: These phrases repeat the original idea but start on different beats in the bar. From bar 52, the two-bar loop is running, so you will be coming in halfway through the loop, or just at the end, and going over into the next loop. None of this really matters if you just leave the overdub function running. Just count out the rests, play through everything as written and it should all work out fine!

To help illustrate how the piece is constructed (and what you can expect to hear), the playback part is included in smaller dots in the notation, so you can see how the live and recorded layers interact.

Bar 64: These slapped harmonics are meant to imitate the "prepared guitar" sound of Glenn Branca or Ex-Easter Island Head but without extra equipment. Hammer down the fretting hand against the fret-wire and quickly bounce off the strings to generate the harmonics. A tremolo pedal would make these stand out nicely.

Bar 70: After a few repetitions, bring the loop to a sudden cut-off as the loop ends, before the next down beat.

Movement III:

Bars 71-72: The third movement features longer loops, as each layer is in a different time signature and the timing loop must be a common multiple of them all. Unlike earlier loops, play the full repeat and only close the loop after four bars of 6/4, then go straight into overdubbing bar 73.

Bar 73: Getting a seamless link from the previous riff into the natural harmonic at the 12th fret without disrupting your groove will take practice. Look ahead to the 12th fret and release the 2nd fret early to jump position on time.

Bar 75: Slap these natural harmonics with the picking hand thumb, but to make them even more percussive and embrace the spirit of the genre, you could have a look for some alternative household utensils like a wooden spoon, plastic ruler, knitting needle or pen...

Bar 81 to End: It's time to get creative with some effects. The simplest way to end is to gradually turn the volume/mix down on your loop pedal, but this can sound a bit simplistic. To make the fade-out more interesting you can put down the guitar and introduce some spatial effects. On the performance, I used a combination of an Earthquaker Devices' *Levitation* (reverb), Electro Harmonix *Freeze,* and an Electro Harmonix *Memory-Man* analogue delay – gradually manipulating the controls while fading out the loop.

Liverpool Counterpoint – Rob Thorpe

Movement I

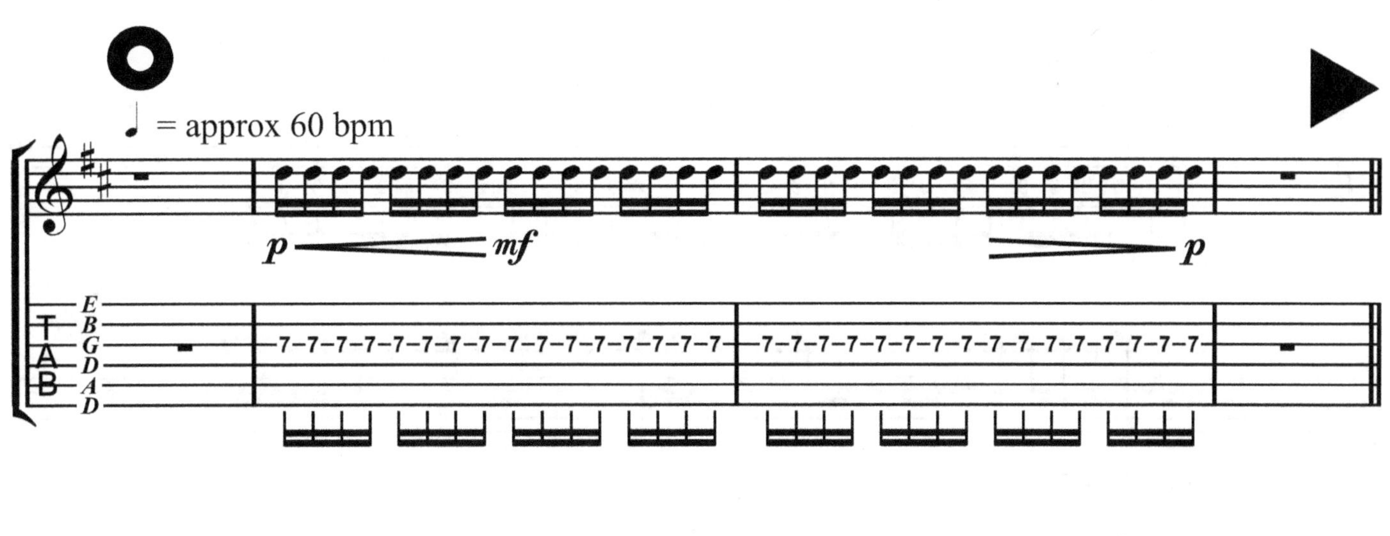

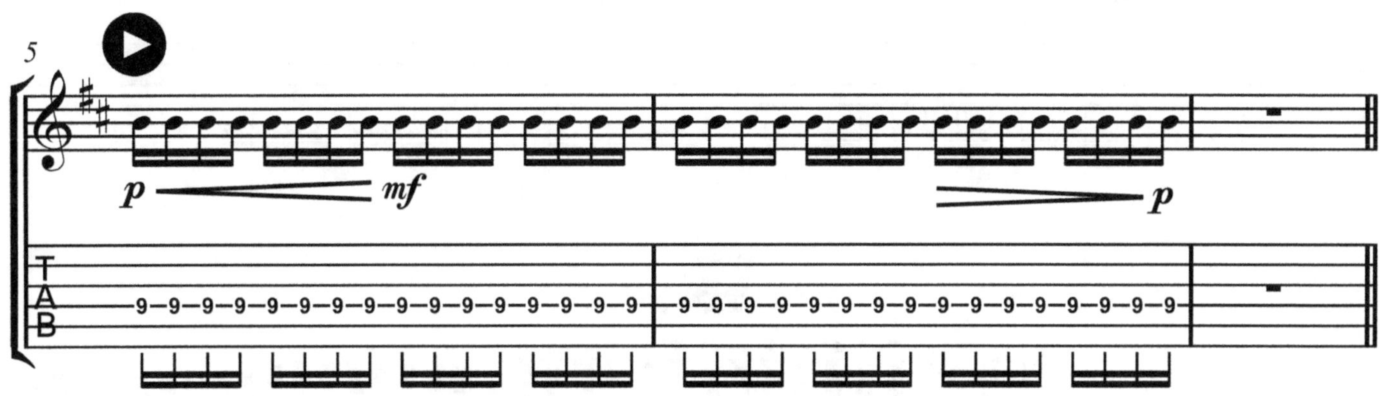

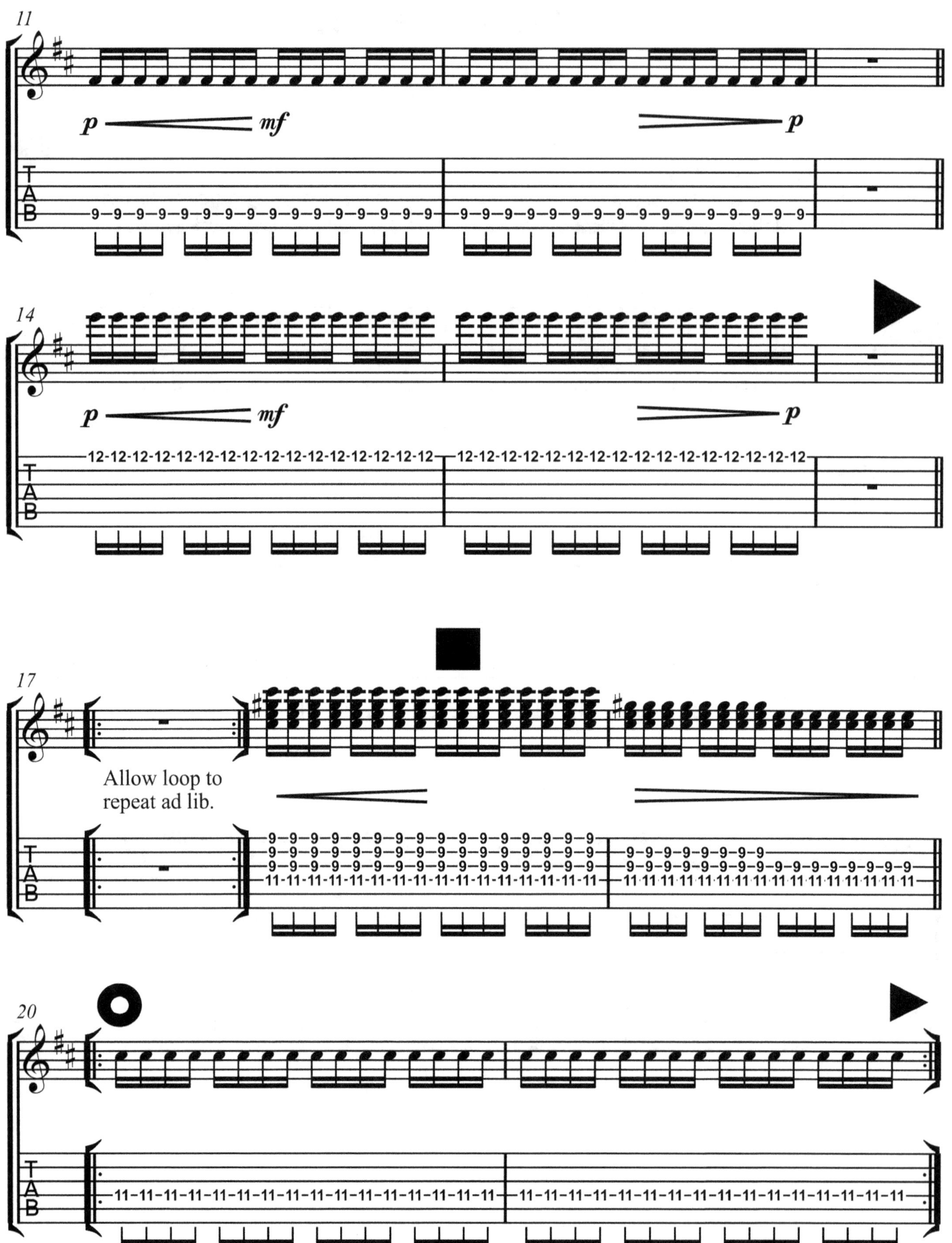

11
p
mf
p
T
A
B
14
p
mf
p
T
A
B
17
Allow loop to repeat ad lib.
T
A
B
20
T
A
B

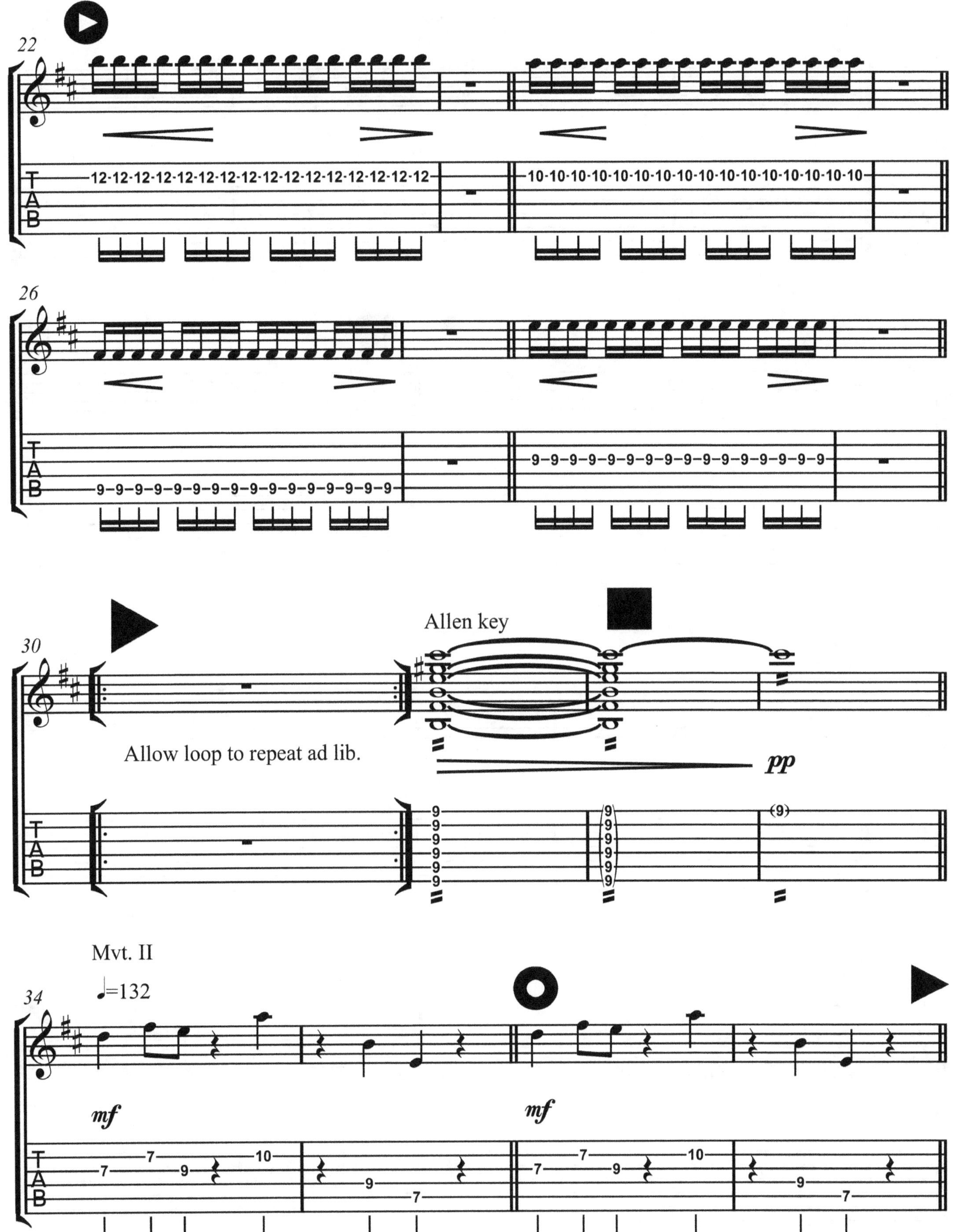
22
26
30
Allen key
Allow loop to repeat ad lib.
pp
Mvt. II
♩=132
34
mf
mf

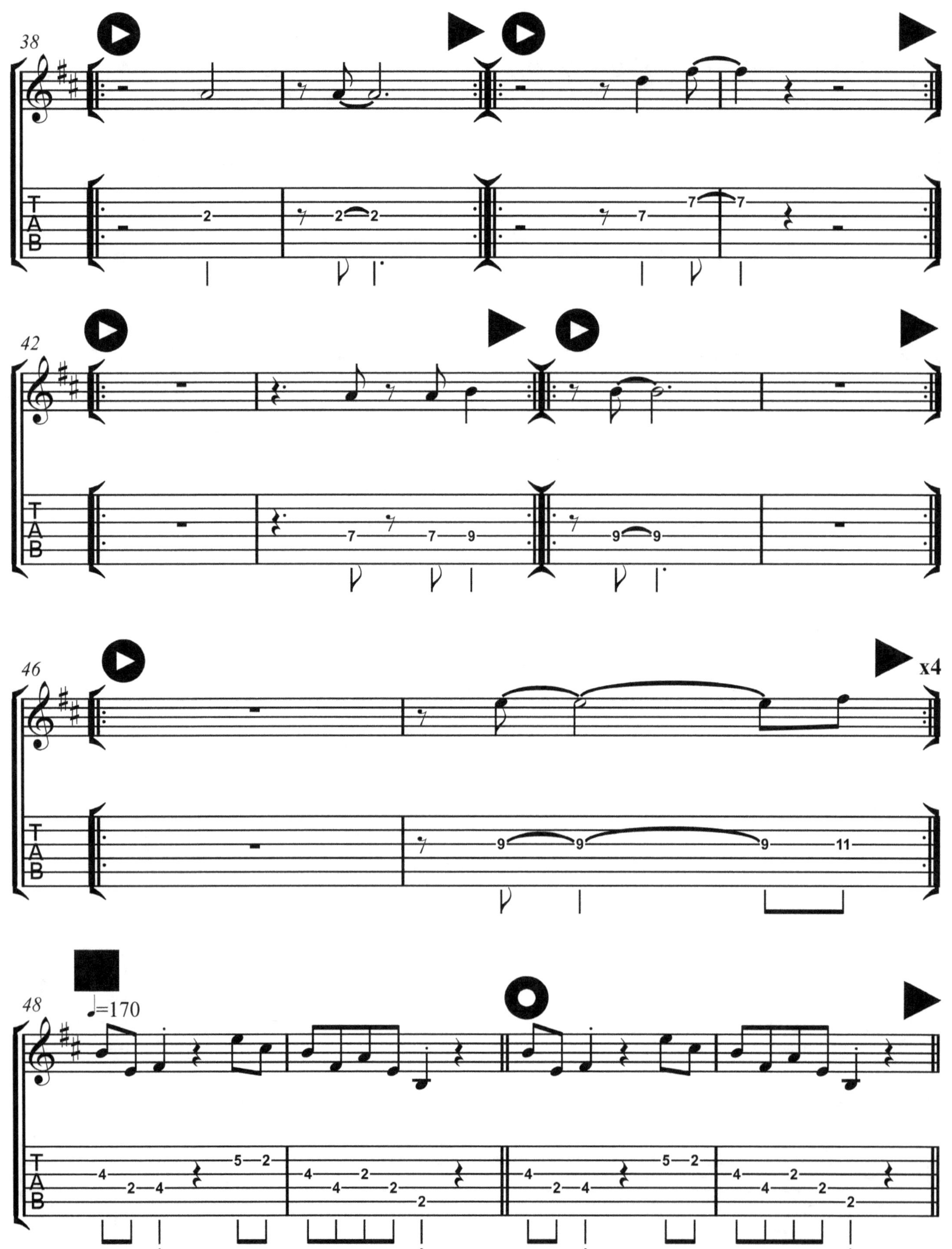
38
42
46
x4
48
♩=170
TAB

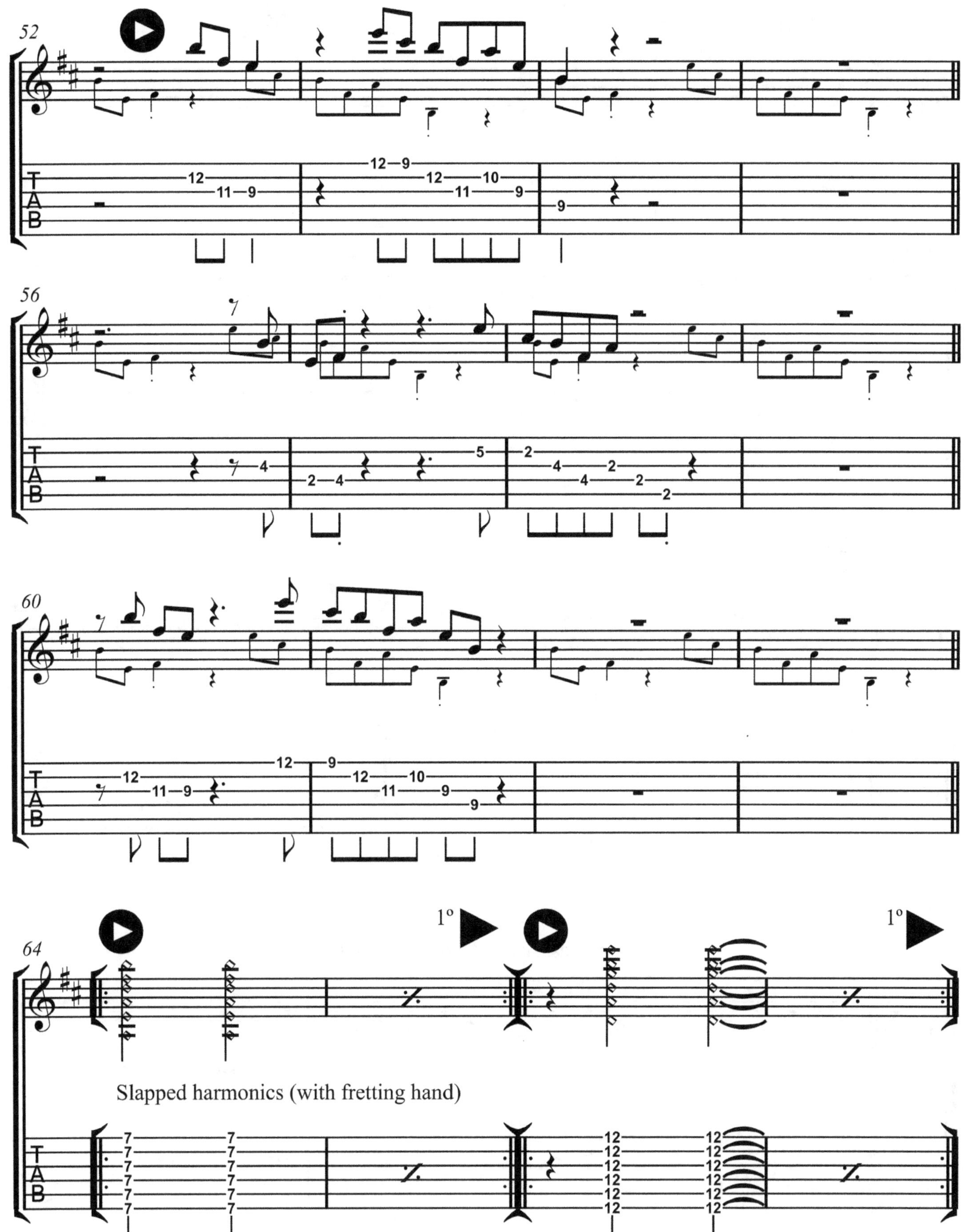
52
56
60
64
1º
1º
Slapped harmonics (with fretting hand)

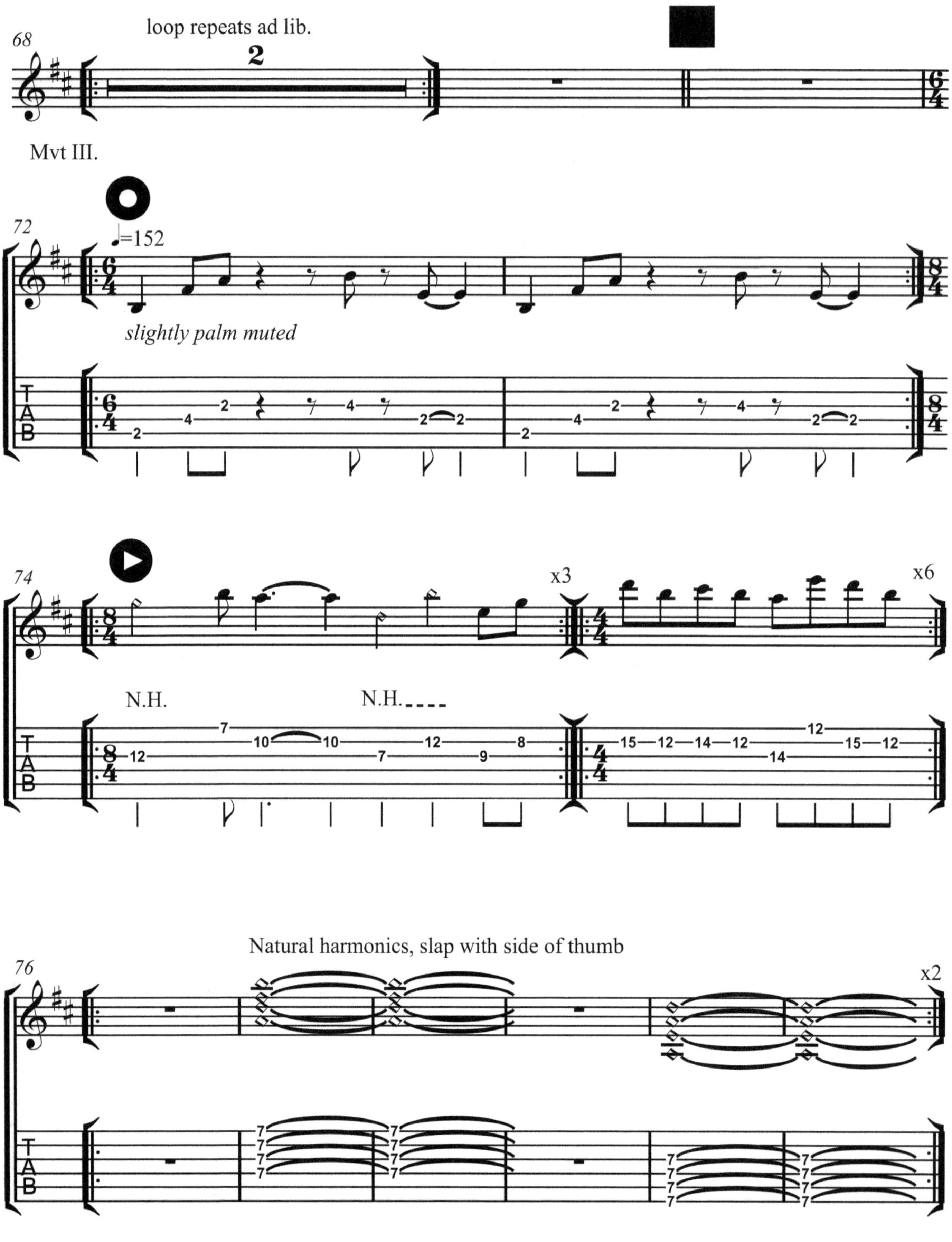

68

loop repeats ad lib.

2

Mvt III.

72

♩=152

slightly palm muted

74

x3

x6

N.H.

N.H.

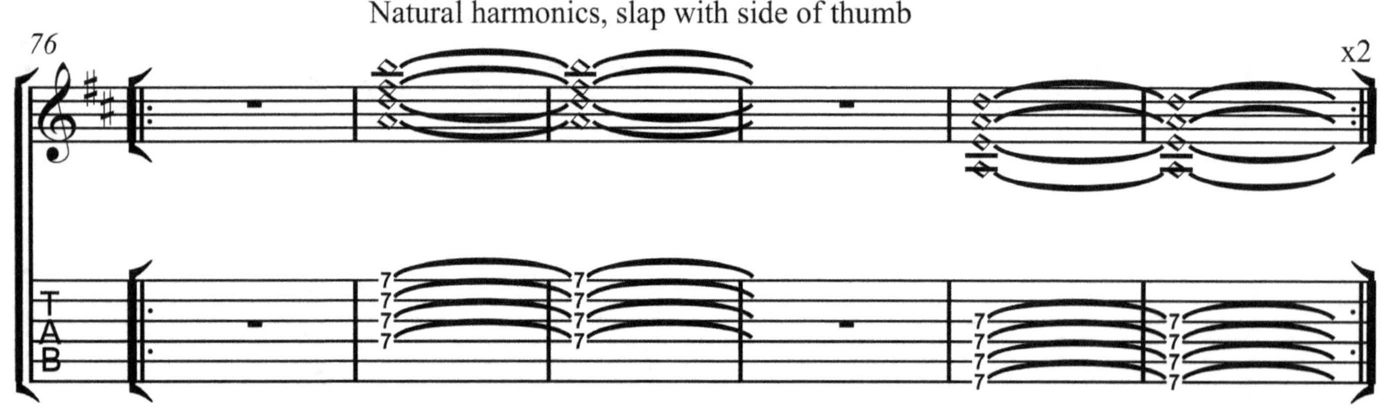

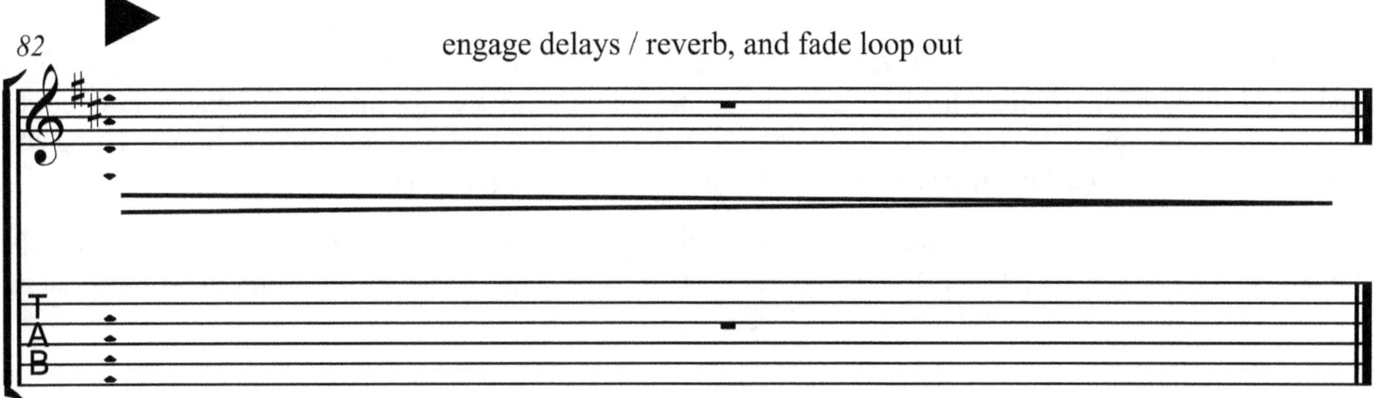
82
engage delays / reverb, and fade loop out
T
A
B

Chapter Eight – *Étude No. 12, Op. 25 "Ocean"* (Frédéric Chopin)

This piece is my take on Chopin's *Étude No. 12, Op. 25*, often called "The Ocean Étude", which was the final etude published during Chopin's lifetime. The energy and colour suggested by this piece's shifting key centres and waves of arpeggios create a sense of rage and pathos. The piece was composed soon after his home city of Warsaw had been attacked by Russia during the November Uprising of 1830-31.

My reworking of Chopin's etude combines his original chord progression with the arpeggio style of the '80s Shrapnel-era guitarists, like Jason Becker and Tony MacAlpine. Most of the piece is played with economy/sweep picking, with some hybrid picking and legato where needed.

Sweep vs. Economy Picking

Most rock guitarists who use sweep picking settle into a few fixed patterns and build their licks around them, while economy picking incorporates those motor skills more naturally into your everyday style.

A full introduction to sweep picking is beyond the space available here, but if you'd like to learn more about its basic mechanics, check out Chris Brooks' *Sweep Picking Speed Strategies for Guitar*.

The first bar shows the typical three-string A minor arpeggio used by rock guitarists. The next two bars take the pattern and apply it to other three-string groups – a simple variation but one that's rarely explored.

Example 8a:

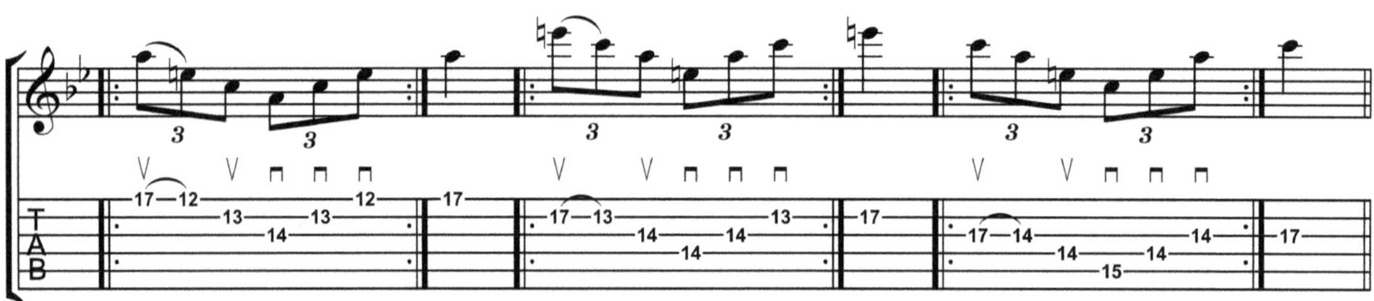

Here's a longer phrase that expands the sweep pattern into an economy-picked approach. Make sure to keep your hand position as consistent as possible to speed up the process of blending the two picking approaches.

Example 8b:

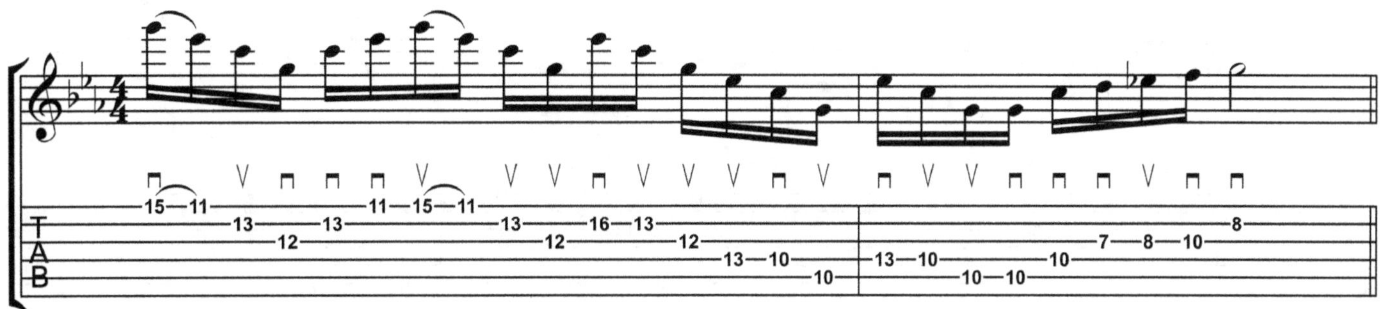

Compare the previous arpeggios with the following scale, which is typical of the kind used in economy picking.

Economy picking one or three notes per string allows you to sweep through the string, while the four notes on the high E help you to turn around and sweep back across with upstrokes.

Example 8c:

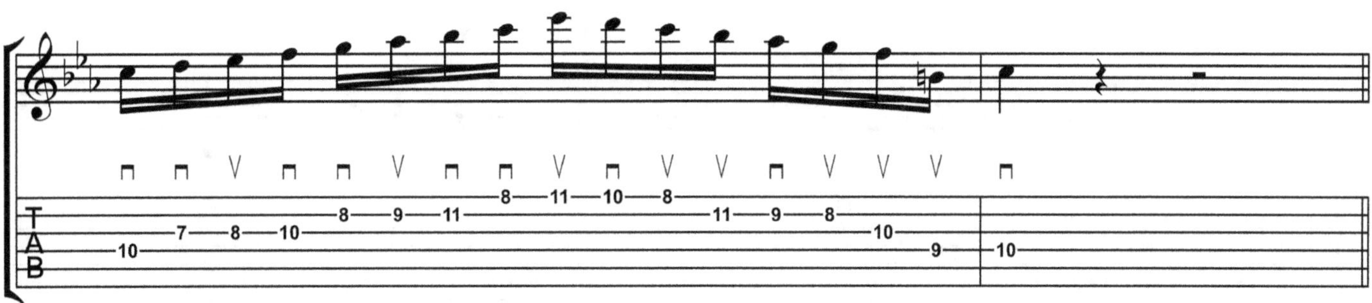

A defining feature of the original piano part is the repeating notes in each arpeggio, which give rhythmic interest and stop the melodic shape from becoming too predictable. The difficulty, compared with Example 8c, is that the pick now needs to continue in the same direction, despite having done an even number of strokes on a string. This requires an inside pick stroke to hook back over the string to reach the next note. Disrupting a sweep stroke in this way is uncommon and playing it cleanly will be this piece's main challenge.

The hooking inside pick stroke lands on the beat, so accent the notes on the E string with some extra twang. Don't worry about economy of motion to begin with, clear and relaxed strokes are more important.

Example 8d:

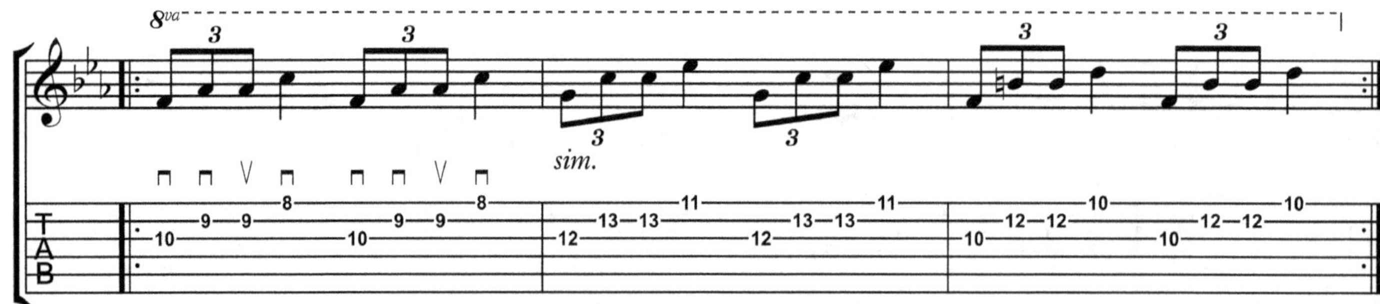

Let's expand Example 8d onto all six strings and continue the sweep after the inside pick stroke following the repeated notes. My own sweeping motion comes from the elbow, so that my hand is always in the same position relative to every string. However, the alternate pick strokes come from the wrist and the resulting technique combines these two movements as smoothly as possible.

Example 8e:

Chopin's Harmony

The harmony in Romantic classical music has been of great inspiration to rock musicians. For example, the band Muse have borrowed from Chopin, Liszt and Rachmaninov to name but a few.

Musical style in Chopin's time still favoured *functional* harmony, where the chords have expected roles in the key and cadences are used to create a sense of tension and release. However, Chopin started to break these expectations by using unrelated chord changes, chosen for their colour rather than their harmonic function.

Examine the following progression and identify any I-V or V-I cadences. Notice any chords that are unrelated to the ones preceding them, which should stand out easily when listening to the audio.

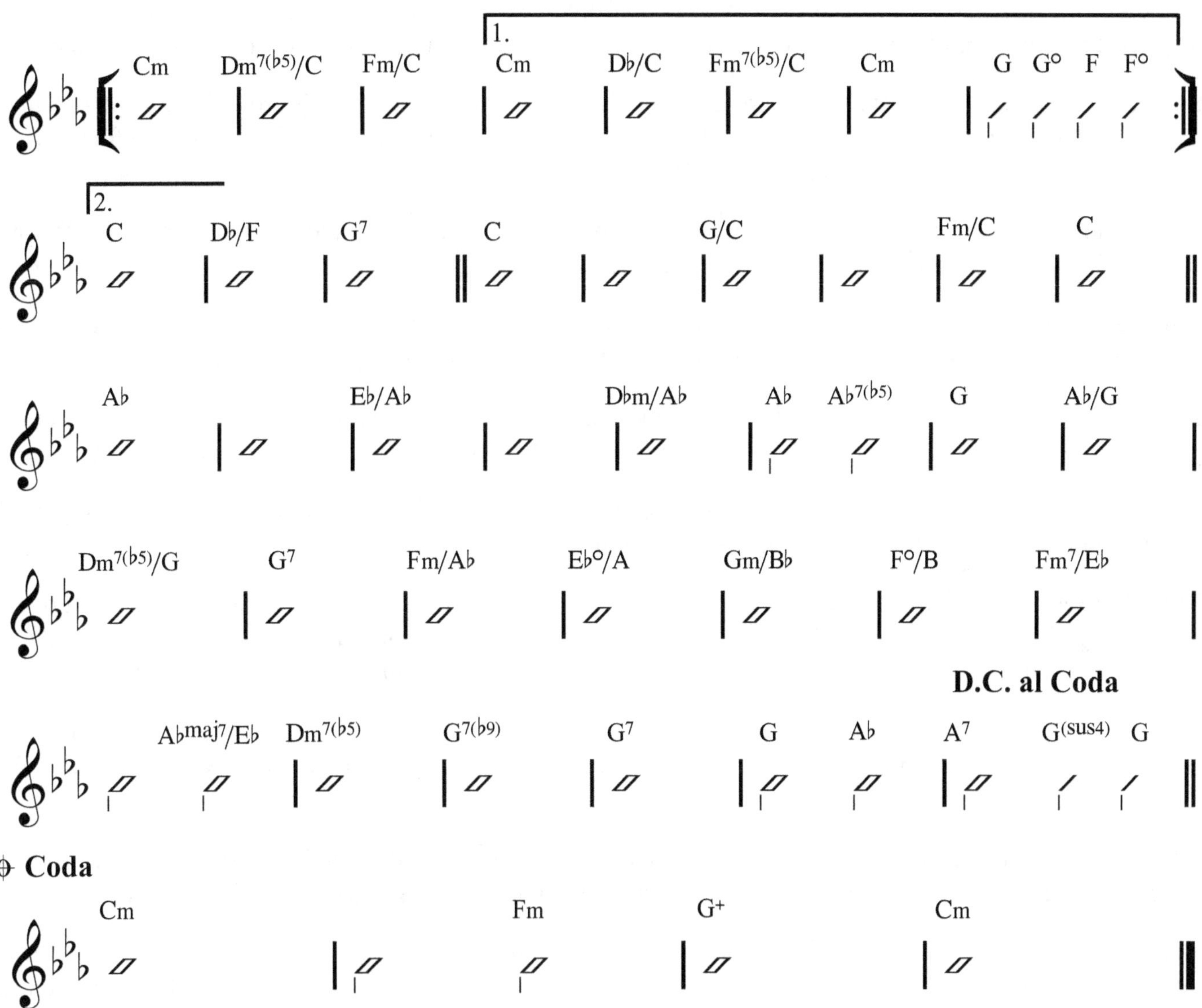

Playing Notes:

Bars 1-2: The first two bars use similar picking patterns, which you should practice at a moderate tempo before tackling the rest of the piece. The Dm7b5 arpeggio is a less common shape and uses the weaker fingers. If the third finger has trouble rolling between the G and B strings use some palm muting to tidy things up.

Bar 3: Here is the first use of repeated notes within an arpeggio. This is an uncommon picking technique that produces a unique rhythmic contour. Follow the picking directions carefully and aim for as little movement as possible in the picking hand. It might feel awkward and unfamiliar to start with, but the interesting contour it adds is worth the effort.

Bar three also features some tricky fingerings for the fretting hand. Two notes at the same fret on adjacent strings can be played with a barre-roll. If that's a challenge, use two different fingers but be sure to shift the whole fretting hand slightly up the neck as you swap from one to the other. Similarly, use your second followed by your third finger on the middle two strings at the 10th fret, then shift position back down the fretboard.

Bar 8: Your picking hand gets a rest here as you only pick the first note of each group before the remainder are played legato. The hammer-on from nowhere on the A string should be done with a flattened finger, which mutes the D and E strings as it lands.

Bars 9-10: Wherever possible, each arpeggio shape follows the same basic layout, so learning these few bars thoroughly means that the later shapes will feel somewhat familiar.

Bars 12-21: These two-bar arpeggios start with sweep picking before moving to hybrid picking for the last three beats. Hammer on all the notes in beat 1 of bar 13 to give your picking hand time to reset.

Bar 23: This Ab7b5 contains Ab, Ebb (D), C, and Gb (F#), which can be seen as a D7b5 chord creating a perfect cadence into the subsequent G major chord. This is known as a *tritone substitution*.

Bar 24: This G major arpeggio contains many open strings, which gives a more country-style twang on the repeated notes and provides a short break from the intricate sweep picking.

Bar 34: Follow the picking directions here. The Ab in beat 2 is hammered to give the pick time to get over to the E string. Beats 3-4 use slightly faster quintuplet rhythms, but don't worry about getting these exact. Chopin would often write long phrases of odd-numbered tuplets that were meant as a slight burst of extra speed and energy.

Bar 36: The next couple of bars are best tackled with hybrid picking. Use alternate down picks and middle finger throughout.

Bar 37: The first two notes of this G7 arpeggio are tricky to finger. Roll the first finger from tip to pad as usual but bring the picking hand further across to palm mute the bottom two strings.

Bar 40: This closing phrase is a big triumphant cadenza and should come crashing down onto the heavy descending quavers. Practice it evenly at a variety of tempos before working on a controlled acceleration and deceleration.

Étude No. 12, Op. 25 "Ocean" – F. Chopin, arr. by Rob Thorpe

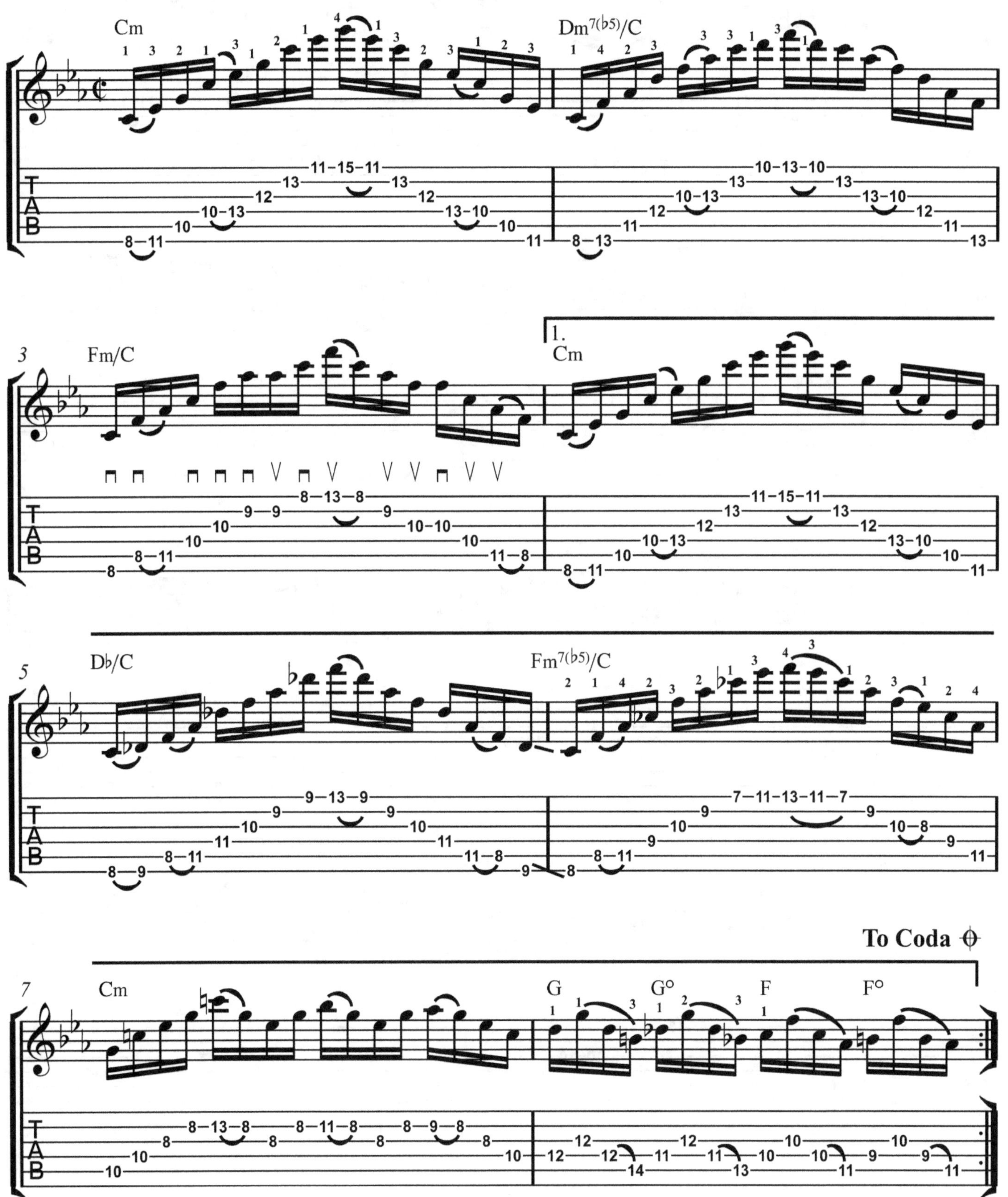

2.
C
D♭/F
G7
C
G/C
Fm/C
C

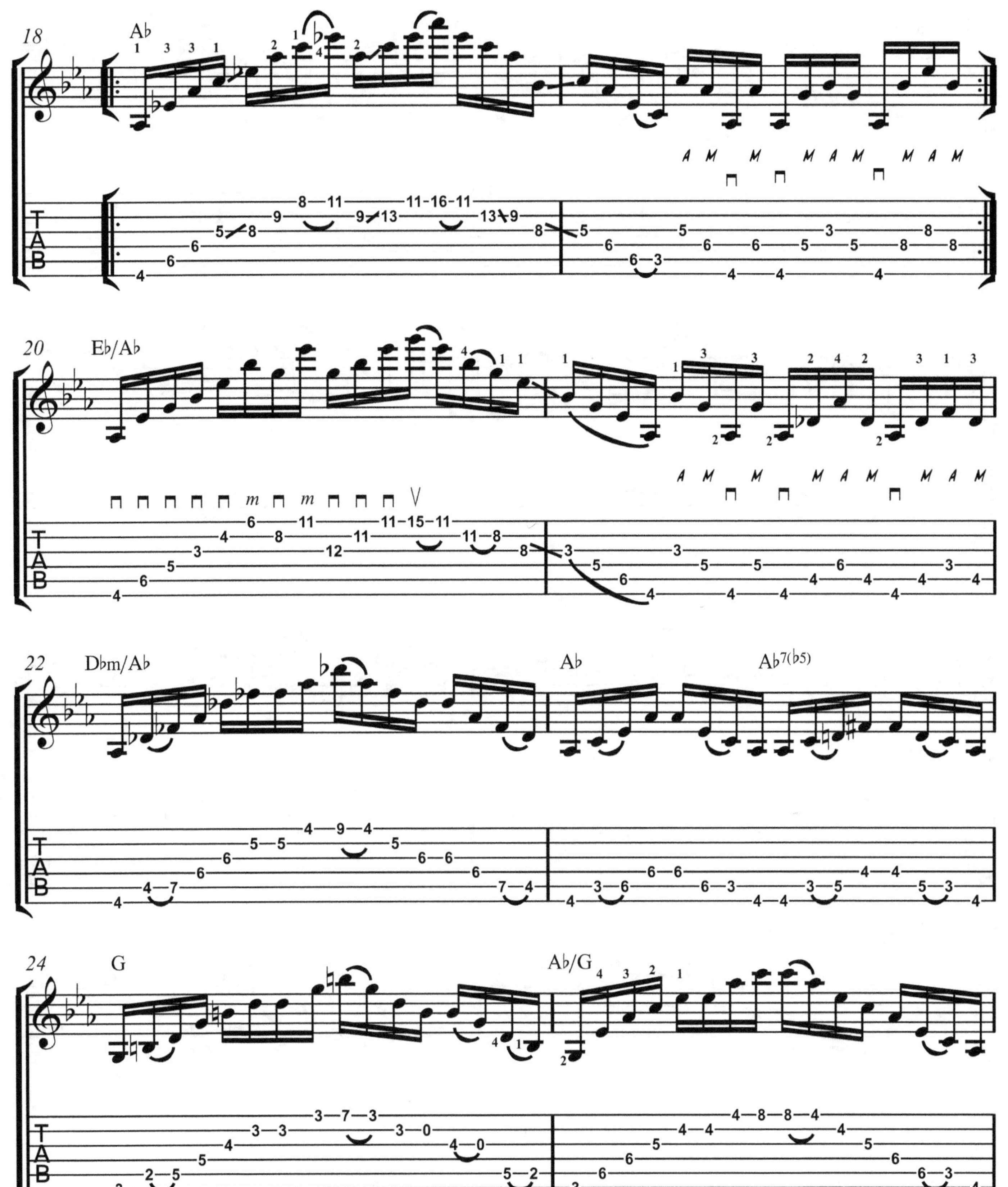
18
A♭
20
E♭/A♭
22
D♭m/A♭
A♭
A♭7(♭5)
24
G
A♭/G

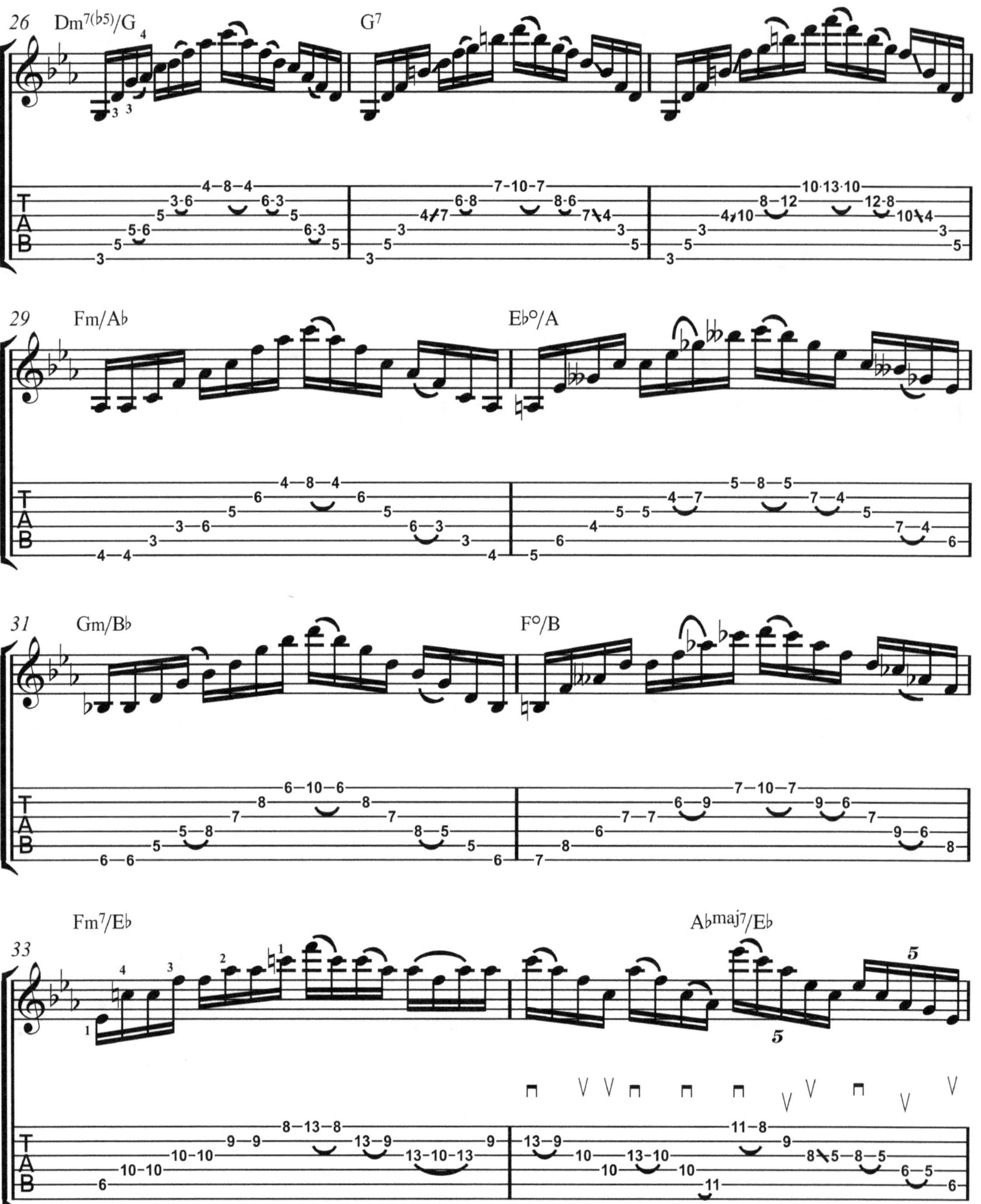
26
Dm7(♭5)/G
G7
29
Fm/A♭
E♭o/A
31
Gm/B♭
Fo/B
33
Fm7/E♭
A♭maj7/E♭
TAB

35
Dm7(♭5)
G7(♭9)
G7
D.C. al Coda
38
G
A♭
A7
G(sus4)
G
Coda
Cm
8va
Fm
40
42
G+
C
P.M.

Closing Words

Phew! You've made it!

Whether you've learned one piece from this or soldiered on right through the book, it's a serious achievement, and hopefully you feel the benefit to your playing.

These challenging pieces test a wide range of techniques and demand disciplined practice, but they also offer many rewards for musicianship and provide you with a unique solo repertoire.

Mastering these pieces is a long-term challenge. Once the technique and execution are consistent then you can make more expressive and creative choices that personalise your interpretation. Later, revisiting these pieces will provide an opportunity for reinterpretation. For instance, I've known Bach's *B Minor Violin Partita* for close to 15 years but almost every time I play it, I discover new details to highlight.

There's great benefit in studying the compositions for their harmony, structure and melodic shape. If you are interested in writing music or developing a unique soloing style, then listen to the pieces and focus on understanding the parts that particularly appeal to you. I've especially enjoyed weaving some of Paganini's arpeggio phrases into my metal solos.

If you're wondering where to go next, try writing your own music or arranging a piece of classical music for electric guitar. There is great scope to discover previously untravelled paths.

I'm excited to hear how you get on, so please tag me in your practice or performance videos.

IG/Facebook/YouTube:

@robthorpemusic

IG: @fundamentalchanges

facebook.com/groups/fundamentalguitar

Best of luck with your journey, intrepid guitarists!

Rob

Recommended Listening

The importance of dedicated listening to our musical development is always overshadowed by the (perceived) more proactive instrumental practice or study of theory. However, it's worth remembering that all the answers lie in the music itself. I heartily recommend listening as widely and openly as possible, exploring the vast interconnected web of music from around the world, both past and contemporary.

I have collected a diverse range of solo and ensemble guitar recordings. These recordings range from shred/rock to jazz, contemporary classical, ambient, and experimental music, but they all expand the role of the electric guitar beyond its scope as a blues-rock band instrument.

Hearing the electric guitar in this unusual and spacious context provides greater scope to explore new textures and ways of playing, which may spark inspiration that you can take back to playing in a band.

Joe Satriani – *Midnight* (1986), *Day at the Beach* (1989) and *Bamboo* (2004)

Joe Pass – *Virtuoso* (1973)

Jeff Parkes – *Forfolk* (2021)

Steve Reich – *Electric Counterpoint* (1987) [performed by Pat Metheny]

Oren Ambarchi – *Simian Angel* (2019)

Fausto Romitelli – *Trash TV Trance* (2002)

Roger Clark Miller – *Eight Dream Interpretations for Solo Electric Guitar Ensemble* (2022)

Mauricio Pauly – *Sky Destroys Dog* (2014) [performed by Daniel Brew of Distractfold]

Ex-Easter Island Head – *Twenty-two Strings* (2020)

Jaco Pastorius – *Portraits of Tracy* (1976)

Nate Chivers – *Nowhere to Hide* (2021)

ELDA ft. Anton Hunter – *Metal Built* (2023)

Hungría – *Cumbre de Nieves Perpetuas*, (2019)

Steve Lawson – *Grace and Gratitude* (2004)

Martyn Heyne – *Eight Reflections in Darkness* (2023)

Emma Ruth Rundle – *Electric Guitar 1* (2014) and *EG2: Dowsing Voice* (2022)

A Lost Coastline – *A Lost Coastline* (2020)

Ben Verdery & Ulysses Quartet – *A Giant Beside You* (2023)

Julien Tassin – *Momentum* (2019)

www.ingramcontent.com/pod-product-compliance
Lightning Source LLC
LaVergne TN
LVHW081253100826
845148LV00009B/1214
9781789334340